Keep it Sim...

140 Simple Calorie Counted Recipes
created for use with
Weight Watchers Quick Start Programme

Weight Watchers *

First Published 1986 by Weight Watchers (U.K.) Ltd.

For information about Weight Watchers classes, contact:

Weight Watchers (U.K.) Ltd.,
11/12 Fairacres, Dedworth Road,
Windsor, Berkshire SL4 4UY.

Telephone: Windsor 856751

Edited by Ann Page-Wood

Cover by Barry Bullough

Illustrations by Jacqueline Weymouth

Contents

About our Recipes

Weight Watchers members enjoy having a varied selection of recipes to use while they follow the Quick Start Programme. This collection of simple recipes has been compiled specially for you, but it can be used by everyone who takes pleasure in good, practical recipes.

- Exchanges are shown so you can fit the recipes into your Weight Watchers Food Plan and we've calorie counted them too.

- Accuracy in weighing ingredients ensures successful results and leads to good weight control.

- Use either the imperial or metric measurements – don't mix the two.
  1 teaspoon=5ml
  1 tablespoon=15ml

- Make sure ingredients measured with a spoon are levelled by using the back of a knife.

- Drain canned fish thoroughly.

- Canned fruit should be in natural juice with no added sugar.

- Buy the leanest joints and cuts of meat.

- Remove skin from poultry before cooking whenever possible.

Happy cooking!

Soups

Cauliflower and Tomato Soup

Serves 4   **30 Calories per serving**

1lb (480g) cauliflower, broken into florets
8fl oz (240ml) tomato juice
¾ pint (450ml) chicken stock, made with stock cube
6oz (180g) mushrooms, sliced
½ teaspoon dried basil
salt and pepper to taste
large sprig parsley, chopped

1) Put the cauliflower in a saucepan with the tomato juice and stock.
2) Bring to the boil, cover, reduce the heat and simmer until tender, about 15 minutes.
3) Cool slightly and put into the blender with the mushrooms. Blend until smooth.
4) Return to the pan add the basil and bring to the boil, simmer for 3 minutes. Adjust the seasoning and serve sprinkled with parsley.

NB This soup will keep for up to 3 days in the refrigerator.

Exchanges per serving: 2 Vegetable
¼ Fruit

Cauliflower Soup

Serves 2   **250 Calories per serving**

½ medium cauliflower, broken into florets
8fl oz (240ml) boiling water
1 medium onion, chopped
3oz (90g) potato, chopped
8fl oz (240ml) skimmed milk
4 teaspoons plain flour
½-1 teaspoon salt
pinch white pepper
pinch grated nutmeg
2oz (60g) Cheddar cheese, grated
1 tablespoon chopped fresh parsley

1) Cook the cauliflower in the boiling water until cooked but still crisp. Drain and reserve the water and the cauliflower.
2) Place the onion and potato in a saucepan, cover with the reserved water and cook for 6-7 minutes until the potato is firm but cooked.
3) In a small bowl gradually blend the milk into the flour. Mix the flour and milk into the potato mixture, stirring all the time. Season with salt, pepper and nutmeg.
4) Bring to the boil, stirring continuously, reduce the heat and simmer gently for 5-10 minutes until the liquid is smooth and thick.
5) Stir in the cauliflower and cheese and cook until the cauliflower has heated through and the cheese melted. Ladle into warm bowls and serve sprinkled with parsley.

Exchanges per serving: 2 Vegetable
½ Bread
¼ Milk
1 Protein
35 Optional Calories

Easy Vegetable Soup

Serves 4   **30 Calories per serving**

8oz (240g) white cabbage, shredded
2 sticks celery, chopped
1 medium cauliflower, chopped
1½ pints (900ml) beef stock,
   made with stock cubes
2oz (60g) courgettes, chopped
2oz (60g) mushrooms, chopped
1 bay leaf
½ teaspoon dried dill
1 garlic clove, crushed, optional
salt to taste

1) Put all the ingredients in a saucepan and bring to the boil.
2) Cover the pan reduce the heat and simmer gently for about 45 minutes.
3) Remove the bay leaf, adjust the seasoning and serve piping hot either with the vegetables as they are or purée in the blender.

NB This soup will keep for up to 3 days in the refrigerator.

Exchanges per serving: 2½ Vegetable

Special Onion Soup

Serves 4   **250 Calories per serving**

2 pints (1 litre 200ml) beef stock,
   made with stock cubes
12oz (360g) onions, thinly sliced
4 x ½oz (4 x 15g) slices French bread, toasted
4oz (120g) mozzarella cheese, shredded
4oz (120g) Parmesan cheese, grated

1) Heat the stock and onions in a saucepan, bring to the boil, reduce the heat and simmer 15-20 minutes.
2) Place the slices of toasted bread into four flameproof dishes, pour a quarter of the soup into each bowl. Sprinkle each portion with 1oz (30g) mozzarella cheese and 1oz (30g) Parmesan cheese.
3) Transfer the soup bowls to a preheated grill and grill 4-5 minutes until the cheese has melted and lightly browned.

Exchanges per serving: 2 Protein
                       1 Vegetable
                       ½ Bread

Leek and Carrot Soup

Serves 4   **45 Calories per serving**

2½ pints (1 litre 500ml) chicken
  stock, made with stock cubes
12oz (360g) trimmed leeks, chopped
12oz (360g) carrots, sliced
¼ teaspoon ground nutmeg
2 bay leaves
¼ teaspoon dried rosemary
salt and pepper to taste

1) Place the stock, vegetables, nutmeg, bay leaves and
   rosemary in a saucepan. Bring to the boil, reduce the
   heat, cover and simmer until the vegetables are tender,
   about 25 minutes.
2) Remove the bay leaves. Transfer the soup to a blender and
   blend until smooth.
3) Adjust the seasoning and serve.

NB This soup will keep for up to 4 days in the refrigerator.

Exchanges per serving: 2 Vegetable

Mushroom Quickie

Serves 4   **55 Calories per serving**

4 teaspoons margarine
1 large onion, chopped
1 garlic clove, crushed
12oz (360g) mushrooms, chopped
¾ pint (450ml) chicken or vegetable
  stock, made with stock cube
1 teaspoon salt
¼ teaspoon dried oregano
pinch white pepper

1) Heat the margarine in a large saucepan until bubbly and
   hot; add the chopped onion and garlic. Sauté until the
   onion is transparent.
2) Stir in the mushrooms and cook, stirring occasionally,
   until all the liquid has evaporated and the mushrooms
   are beginning to brown.
3) Stir in the stock and seasonings, bring to the boil. Reduce
   the heat, cover and simmer for 30 minutes.

NB This soup will keep for up to 3 days in the refrigerator.

Exchanges per serving: 1½ Vegetable
                        1 Fat

Beansprout Soup

Serves 4   **75 Calories per serving**

2 sticks celery, finely chopped
1½ pints (900ml) chicken stock,
    made with stock cubes
1lb (480g) beansprouts
8fl oz (240ml) tomato juice
6oz (180g) cauliflower florets
¼ teaspoon mixed spice
salt and pepper to taste
6oz (180g) cooked small pasta

1) Place all the ingredients except the pasta in a saucepan.
2) Bring to the boil, reduce the heat, cover the pan and simmer for 1 hour, stirring occasionally. Stir in the pasta and reheat.

NB This soup will keep for up to 3 days in the refrigerator.

Exchanges per serving: 2 Vegetable
                        ¼ Fruit
                        ½ Bread

Watercress Soup

Serves 2   **110 Calories per serving**

6oz (180g) watercress
6oz (180g) potato, chopped
12fl oz (360ml) chicken stock,
    made with a stock cube
¼ pint (150ml) skimmed milk
salt and ground black pepper to taste

1) Wash the watercress, cut off discoloured ends of the stems, reserve two sprigs and chop the remainder. Place the watercress and potato in a saucepan with the stock. Bring to the boil and simmer for 15-20 minutes or until the potato is tender.
2) Transfer to blender and purée until smooth.
3) Return to the saucepan, add the milk and reheat without boiling.
4) Adjust the seasoning and serve either piping hot or chilled, garnished with reserved sprigs of watercress.

Exchanges per serving: 1 Vegetable
                        1 Bread
                        ¼ Milk

Meal in a Pot

Serves 2   **220 Calories per serving**

1 teaspoon vegetable oil
1 small onion, chopped
1 medium carrot, finely chopped
1 stick celery, chopped
1 small green or red pepper,
    seeded and chopped
2oz (60g) aubergine, chopped
1 medium tomato, blanched
    peeled and chopped
1 garlic clove, crushed, optional
1 pint (600ml) water
2oz (60g) uncooked lentils, rinsed
2oz (60g) frankfurters, sliced
1 chicken stock cube
1 tablespoon chopped parsley
salt and pepper to taste

1) Heat the oil in a large saucepan. Add the onion, carrot, celery, green or red pepper, aubergine, tomato and garlic and cook, stirring constantly, until the onion is transparent.
2) Add the remaining ingredients and stir well. Simmer over a low heat, stirring occasionally, until the vegetables and lentils are tender, 30-35 minutes.

Exchanges per serving: 2 Protein
                        2½ Vegetable
                        ½ Fat

Pasta and Bean Soup

Serves 2   **140 Calories per serving**

4oz (120g) drained canned
    tomatoes, chopped
1 small carrot, sliced
1 small onion, chopped
1 stick celery, chopped
1 bay leaf
1 pint (600ml) water
3oz (90g) green beans, sliced
2oz (60g) uncooked pasta shapes
2oz (60g) courgettes, sliced
salt and pepper to taste

1) Place the tomatoes, carrot, onion, celery, bay leaf and water in a saucepan, bring to the boil. Reduce the heat and simmer for 15-20 minutes.
2) Add the beans and cook until they are just tender, 8-10 minutes.
3) Add the pasta and courgettes and simmer until the pasta is just cooked.
4) Remove the bay leaf, season with salt and pepper and serve piping hot.

Exchanges per serving: 1 Bread
                        2½ Vegetable

Hearty Beef and Vegetable Soup

Serves 2 **265 Calories per serving**

8oz (240g) braising steak
1½ pints (900ml) water
4fl oz (120ml) mixed vegetable or
  tomato juice
3oz (90g) parsnips, chopped
3oz (90g) turnips, chopped
2oz (60g) cabbage, chopped
1 stick celery, chopped
4 spring onions, chopped
1oz (30g) uncooked lentils, rinsed
½ garlic clove, finely chopped, optional
1oz (30g) mushrooms, sliced
salt and pepper to taste

1) Grill the beef on a rack for 3-5 minutes on each side
   turning once. Cut into 1″ (2.5cm) cubes.
2) Place the beef and all the remaining ingredients in a
   saucepan over a medium heat. Bring to the boil, reduce
   the heat, cover and simmer, stirring occasionally until the
   meat is tender and the vegetables cooked, 45-50 minutes.

Exchanges per serving: 3½ Protein
                        ¼ Fruit
                        2 Vegetable

Pork and Sweetcorn Soup

Serves 1 **295 Calories per serving**

2oz (60g) cooked pork, minced
1 tablespoon soy sauce
1 teaspoon cornflour
¾ pint (450ml) water
¾″ (2cm) piece of root ginger, peeled
½-1 beef stock cube, crumbled
3oz (90g) drained canned sweetcorn
1 egg, well beaten
2 teaspoons chopped chives

1) Mix together the pork, soy sauce and cornflour. Leave to
   stand in the cool for 10 minutes.
2) Combine the water, ginger and stock cube in a saucepan.
   Bring to the boil over a medium heat, simmer for
   10 minutes; remove and discard the ginger.
3) Stir the pork mixture into the hot stock, simmer for
   5 minutes, stirring occasionally.
4) Add the egg by pouring it down the prongs of a fork into
   the simmering soup.
5) Ladle the soup into a warm soup bowl and sprinkle with
   the chopped chives.

Exchanges per serving: 3 Protein
                        1 Bread
                        10 Optional Calories

Versatile Lentil Soup

Serves 6　　　　　　　　**105 Calories per serving**

6oz (180g) uncooked lentils, rinsed
1½ pints (900ml) water
2 pints (1 litre, 200ml) strong beef stock
　　made with stock cubes
2 medium carrots, chopped
1 medium onion, chopped
3oz (90g) courgettes, chopped
3oz (90g) green beans, sliced
2 sticks celery, thinly sliced
2 garlic cloves, crushed
¼ teaspoon pepper
salt to taste

1) Place the lentils and water in a saucepan, bring to the
　　boil, reduce the heat, cover and simmer 30 minutes.
2) Stir the remaining ingredients into the lentils, cover and
　　simmer, stirring occasionally 30-40 minutes until the
　　lentils and vegetables are tender.

Exchanges per serving:　1 Protein
　　　　　　　　　　　　　1 Vegetable

Chilled Artichoke Soup

Serves 4　　　　　　　　**40 Calories per serving**

12oz (360g) canned artichoke
　　hearts, drained
¾ pint (450ml) chicken stock,
　　made with stock cube
¼ teaspoon dried oregano
2 tablespoons lemon juice
½ pint (300ml) skimmed milk
salt to taste
paprika

1) Rinse artichokes thoroughly, place in the blender with
　　the chicken stock and oregano and blend.
2) Stir in the lemon juice and milk and season to taste. Chill.
3) Sprinkle with paprika and serve.

NB This soup will keep for up to 2 days in the refrigerator.

Exchanges per serving:　1 Vegetable
　　　　　　　　　　　　　¼ Milk

Gazpacho

Serves 2   **45 Calories per serving**

1 medium tomato, blanched,
   peeled, seeded and chopped
1 stick celery, chopped
½ green pepper, seeded and chopped
1 small onion, chopped
3oz (90g) cucumber, chopped
5 tablespoons chicken stock,
   made with ½ a stock cube
½ pint (300ml) tomato juice
1 small garlic clove, crushed
4 teaspoons cider vinegar
dash of hot pepper sauce
salt and pepper to taste

1) Place the tomato, celery, half the onion and about a
   quarter of the green pepper in a small bowl, put to one
   side.
2) Place all the remaining vegetables in a blender with the
   stock, tomato juice, garlic, vinegar and hot pepper sauce.
   Blend until smooth.
3) Season the soup with salt and pepper and chill for
   1-2 hours.
4) Ladle the soup into serving bowls and sprinkle with the
   reserved vegetables.

Exchanges per serving: 2 Vegetable
                        ½ Fruit
                        10 Optional Calories

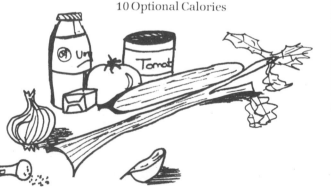

Peanut Butter Soup

Serves 1   **180 Calories per serving**

1 teaspoon oil
2 tablespoons finely chopped onion
1 stick celery, finely chopped
1 tablespoon crunchy peanut butter
8fl oz (240ml) chicken stock,
   made with stock cube
3 medium tomatoes, blanched,
   peeled, seeded and chopped
hot pepper sauce and salt to taste

1) Heat the oil in a saucepan, add the onion and celery.
   Cook, stirring frequently for 2 minutes.
2) Stir in the peanut butter and stock, bring to the boil,
   reduce the heat and simmer, stirring occasionally, for
   8 minutes.
3) Add the tomatoes and return to the boil.
4) Adjust the seasoning according to taste, stir well and
   serve.

Exchanges per serving: 2 Fat
                        4 Vegetable

Traditional Bouillabaisse

Serves 2 **250 Calories per serving**

1 tablespoon olive oil
1 large onion, sliced
1 garlic clove, crushed
14oz (420g) canned tomatoes
6 tablespoons chicken stock, made with ½ a stock cube
2 tablespoons chopped fresh parsley
salt and pepper to taste
1 bouquet garni
6oz (180g) monkfish, cut in chunks
3oz (90g) cod or coley, skinned and cut in chunks
3oz (90g) plaice fillet, skinned
   and cut into 1″ (2.5cm) strips

1) Heat the oil in a saucepan. Sauté the onion and garlic 3-4 minutes.
2) Stir in the tomatoes, chicken stock, 1 tablespoon parsley, salt, pepper and bouquet garni. Bring to the boil, reduce the heat and simmer for 10 minutes.
3) Add the monkfish and simmer for 5 minutes.
4) Stir in the cod or coley and simmer for 4-5 minutes.
5) Stir in the plaice and simmer for a further 3-4 minutes until the plaice is cooked.
6) Remove the bouquet garni, adjust the seasoning and ladle into warm soup bowls. Sprinkle with the remaining parsley and serve immediately.

Exchanges per serving: 1½ Fat
          3 Vegetable
          4½ Protein

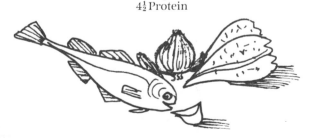

Chicken and Egg Drop Soup

Serves 1 **290 Calories per serving**

3oz (90g) skinned and boned chicken,
   cut into thin shreds
2 teaspoons cornflour
12fl oz (360ml) chicken stock,
   made with a stock cube
¾″ (2cm) piece of root ginger, peeled
3oz (90g) drained canned sweetcorn
1 egg, well beaten
1 tablespoon finely shredded lettuce

1) Place the chicken in the bowl, stir in the cornflour and stir to coat the shreds of the chicken.
2) Gradually bring the stock and ginger to the boil over a medium heat, simmer for 10 minutes; remove and discard the piece of ginger.
3) Stir the coated chicken into the hot stock, cover and simmer for 15 minutes. Stir in the sweetcorn and simmer for a further 2 minutes to heat through.
4) Add the egg by trailing it down the prongs of a fork. Ladle the soup into a warmed soup bowl and garnish with the shredded lettuce.

Exchanges per serving: 3 Protein
          1 Bread
          20 Optional Calories

Salads and Dressings

Index

Basic French Dressing

Serves 2   **90 Calories per serving**

4 teaspoons olive or vegetable oil
2 tablespoons wine vinegar
pinch of salt
pinch of pepper

1) Combine all the ingredients in a jar, cover securely and shake vigorously or mix well in a small basin.

Variations:
This dressing can be adapted in numerous ways to suit various salads. Try adding any of the following:
1 clove garlic, crushed
2 teaspoons chopped fresh chives
2 teaspoons chopped fresh oregano
dash of hot pepper sauce

Exchanges per serving: 2 Fat

Oriental Dressing

Serves 4   **70 Calories per serving**

2 tablespoons peanut or vegetable oil
1 tablespoon rice or cider vinegar
1 tablespoon water
1 tablespoon finely chopped celery
1 tablespoon finely chopped spring onion
2 teaspoons soy sauce
1 teaspoon lime juice
2 teaspoons tomato ketchup
1 thin slice peeled root ginger

1) Place all the ingredients in a blender, blend until smooth scraping down the sides of the container as necessary.

2) Pour the dressing into a container, cover and chill well.

3) Stir well or shake before using, excess dressing may be stored in the refrigerator for up to 4 days.

Exchanges per serving: $1\frac{1}{2}$ Fat
                                 $\frac{1}{4}$ Vegetable
                                 5 Optional Calories

Caper Dressing

Serves 2   **55 Calories per serving**

3 tablespoons low-fat natural yogurt
2 tablespoons low-calorie mayonnaise
1 teaspoon drained chopped capers

1) Combine all the ingredients in a jar, cover securely and shake vigorously or mix well in a small basin.

2) Chill the covered dressing in the refrigerator for at least 30 minutes before serving. Shake or mix well before use.

Exchanges per serving: 1½ Fat
                        15 Optional Calories

Green Mayonnaise

Serves 1   **50 Calories per serving**

1 tablespoon skimmed milk
1 tablespoon low-calorie mayonnaise
1 teaspoon chopped fresh chives
2 tablespoons finely chopped watercress
salt and pepper to taste

1) Gradually blend the skimmed milk into the mayonnaise a few drops at a time.

2) Add the chives and watercress and mix well. Season to taste with salt and pepper.

Exchanges per serving: 1½ Fat
                        ¼ Vegetable
                        5 Optional Calories

Sesame Dressing

Serves 2   **45 Calories per serving**

1½ teaspoons sesame seeds, toasted
3 tablespoons low-fat natural yogurt
1 teaspoon sesame oil
pinch ground cumin
salt and pepper to taste

1) Crush the toasted sesame seeds in a pestle and mortar or by using the end of a rolling pin and pressing against the side of a small basin.
2) Combine the yogurt, sesame seeds, sesame oil and cumin, mix well. Season to taste, cover and chill. Mix once again before use.

Exchanges per serving: ½ Fat
                                30 Optional Calories

Blue Cheese Dressing

Serves 2   **90 Calories per serving**

5fl oz (150ml) low-fat natural yogurt
1oz (30g) blue cheese, crumbled
½ teaspoon wine or cider vinegar
salt and pepper to taste

1) Place all the ingredients in a blender, blend until smooth. Pour the dressing into a container, cover and chill. Stir well before use.

Exchanges per serving: ½ Milk
                                ½ Protein

Pimiento Dressing

Serves 4 **25 Calories per serving**

6oz (180g) canned pimientos, drained
2 tablespoons cider vinegar
2 tablespoons French mustard
2 teaspoons caster sugar

1) Combine all the ingredients in a blender and blend until smooth.

2) Store in a small sealed jar in the refrigerator for up to 5 days.

Exchanges per serving: ½ Vegetable
10 Optional Calories

Chinese Chicken

Serves 2 **245 Calories per serving**

8oz (240g) canned pineapple chunks
with 4 tablespoons juice, reserved
1 tablespoon rice or cider vinegar
1½ teaspoons Dijon-style mustard
1 teaspoon peanut or vegetable oil
dash five-spice powder
6oz (180g) skinned and boned cooked
chicken breasts, cut into thin strips
4oz (120g) crisp lettuce, shredded
4 tablespoons chopped spring onions
2 tablespoons chopped fresh parsley
1 small red pepper, cored,
seeded and sliced
1½oz (45g) drained canned water
chestnuts, sliced
½ teaspoon sesame seeds, toasted

1) Place the reserved pineapple juice, vinegar, mustard, oil and five-spice powder in a jar, cover securely and shake vigorously.

2) Pour the dressing over the chicken strips, cover and chill for at least 1 hour.

3) In a separate bowl mix together the lettuce, spring onions, parsley, red pepper, water chestnuts and pineapple chunks.

4) Line the serving dish with the lettuce mixture, spoon over the chicken and the marinade. Sprinkle with sesame seeds.

Exchanges per serving: 1 Fruit
½ Fat
3 Protein
1½ Vegetable
30 Optional Calories

Turkey Salad

Serves 2   **250 Calories per serving**

6oz (180g) skinned and boned
  cooked turkey
3oz (90g) drained canned
  water chestnuts, sliced
2 sticks celery, chopped
½ medium green pepper,
  seeded and chopped
1 small carrot, grated
4 teaspoons low-calorie mayonnaise
2 large crisp lettuce leaves
2 hard boiled eggs, quartered

1) Cut the turkey into ½" (1cm) cubes.
2) Mix together the turkey, water chestnuts, celery, green
   pepper and carrot. Stir in the mayonnaise and mix well.
3) Lay a lettuce leaf on each serving plate. Pile half the turkey
   salad on top of each leaf garnish with the hard boiled
   eggs.

Exchanges per serving: 4 Protein
                        ½ Bread
                        1½ Vegetable
                        1 Fat

Tuna Salad in Orange Sauce

Serves 2   **315 Calories per serving**

2 medium oranges
6oz (180g) drained canned
  tuna, flaked
2 sticks celery, thinly sliced
2 tablespoons chopped cucumber
1 tablespoon chopped spring onion
½ medium red pepper,
  seeded and chopped
2 hard boiled eggs, chopped
1½ teaspoons Worcestershire sauce
1 tablespoon tomato purée
2 tablespoons low-calorie mayonnaise
salt and pepper to taste
2 large crisp lettuce leaves

1) Cut the top third off each orange, the larger pieces will
   form the bowl to hold the salad. Carefully scoop out the
   flesh from both oranges, top and bottom, take care not to
   cut through the peel. Cut the flesh into large pieces
   removing any loose membranes.
2) Combine the tuna, celery, cucumber, spring onion, red
   pepper and chopped eggs, mix well.
3) Mix the Worcestershire sauce, tomato purée and
   mayonnaise well together. Stir into the tuna mixture with
   the orange pieces. Season to taste.
4) Lay a lettuce leaf on each serving plate. Divide the salad
   between the orange bowls and serve on the lettuce leaves.

Exchanges per serving: 1 Fruit
                        4 Protein
                        1½ Vegetable
                        1½ Fat
                        5 Optional Calories

Coleslaw

Serves 2   **110 Calories per serving**

8oz (240g) white cabbage, finely shredded
4oz (120g) red cabbage, finely shredded
1oz (30g) carrot, grated
1 stick celery, chopped
½ medium green pepper, seeded and chopped
2 tablespoons chopped spring onions
2″ (5cm) chunk cucumber, chopped
2 radishes, thinly sliced
4 tablespoons low-fat natural yogurt
3-4 teaspoons red wine vinegar
2 teaspoons olive or vegetable oil
½ clove garlic, crushed

1) Mix the white and red cabbages, carrot, celery, green pepper, spring onions, cucumber and radishes together in a large bowl.
2) Place all the remaining ingredients in a jar, cover securely and shake vigorously.
3) Pour the dressing over the cabbage mixture and toss well to coat. Cover and chill until ready to serve. Toss once again.

Exchanges per serving: 3 Vegetable
                      1 Fat
                      20 Optional Calories

Waldorf Style Salad

Serves 2   **105 Calories per serving**

1 medium red apple, quartered, cored and chopped
1 tablespoon lemon juice
2 sticks celery, chopped
1oz (30g) seedless raisins
4 teaspoons low-calorie mayonnaise
2 large crisp lettuce leaves, shredded
2 teaspoons sunflower seeds

1) Toss the apple in the lemon juice in a bowl.
2) Add the celery, raisins and low-calorie mayonnaise, mix well. Cover and chill for at least 30 minutes.
3) Line two serving glasses or bowls with the shredded lettuce. Stir the apple and celery mixture well and spoon on top of the lettuce. Sprinkle with sunflower seeds and serve.

Exchanges per serving: 1 Fruit
                      ½ Vegetable
                      1 Fat
                      20 Optional Calories

Special Spinach Salad

Serves 1   **165 Calories per serving**

2oz (60g) spinach leaves,
   torn or roughly chopped
1oz (30g) crisp lettuce leaves,
   torn or roughly chopped
1oz (30g) mushrooms, sliced
1 medium tomato, blanched,
   peeled and chopped
4 tablespoons low-fat
   natural yogurt
$\frac{1}{2}$ teaspoon Dijon-style mustard
$\frac{1}{2}$ teaspoon clear honey
pinch ground ginger
salt and pepper to taste
1 hard boiled egg, chopped

1) Mix the spinach, lettuce, mushrooms and tomato
   together in a bowl.
2) Place the yogurt, mustard, honey, ginger and seasoning
   in a jar, cover securely and shake vigorously.
3) Pour the dressing over the spinach salad and toss well.
4) Pile the salad on to a serving plate and sprinkle over the
   chopped egg.

Exchanges per serving: 2 Vegetable
                        1 Protein
                        50 Optional Calories

Herb Marinated Tomatoes

Serves 2   **55 Calories per serving**

2 medium tomatoes, sliced
4 teaspoons red wine vinegar
2 teaspoons olive or vegetable oil
$\frac{1}{4}$ teaspoon salt
pinch mustard powder
$\frac{1}{2}$ teaspoon chopped fresh tarragon leaves
$\frac{1}{2}$ teaspoon chopped fresh oregano leaves
$\frac{1}{2}$ teaspoon chopped fresh thyme leaves
2 large crisp lettuce leaves

1) Arrange the tomato slices in a shallow dish – do not use
   metal or this may cause the flavour to deteriorate.
2) In a small bowl mix together the vinegar, oil, salt,
   mustard and herbs, pour over the tomato slices, cover
   and chill for at least 1 hour basting the tomato several
   times with the marinade.
3) Lay the lettuce leaves on the serving plate and top with the
   tomato slices and marinade.

Exchanges per serving: 1 Fat
                        $1\frac{1}{2}$ Vegetable

Greek Salad

Serves 2　　　　　**230 Calories per serving**

4oz (120g) crisp lettuce,
　　torn or shredded
6oz (180g) drained canned
　　chick peas
1 medium tomato, cut into wedges
¼ medium cucumber, thinly sliced
½ medium green pepper,
　　seeded and thinly sliced
12 stoned black olives, sliced
2oz (60g) feta cheese, crumbled
1 tablespoon olive oil
2 teaspoons drained capers
1 teaspoon white wine vinegar
1 teaspoon lemon juice
½ teaspoon chopped fresh dill
sprig of dill

1) Mix together the lettuce, chick peas, tomato, cucumber,
　　green pepper, olives and feta cheese.
2) Place all the remaining ingredients, except the sprig of
　　dill in a jar, cover securely and shake vigorously.
3) Pour the dressing over the salad and toss well to coat.
　　Serve garnished with the sprig of dill.

Exchanges per serving:　2 Vegetable
　　　　　　　　　　　2 Protein
　　　　　　　　　　　1½ Fat
　　　　　　　　　　　30 Optional

Savoury Banana Salad

Serves 1　　　　　**135 Calories per serving**

½ medium orange, cut lengthways
1oz (30g) crisp lettuce, shredded
4 tablespoons alfalfa sprouts
½ medium banana
1 teaspoon lemon juice
2oz (60g) cottage cheese
1 teaspoon sunflower seeds

1) Using a potato peeler cut a 2″ (5cm) strip from the orange,
　　cut into matchstick size strips and reserve for garnish.
　　Remove the remaining peel with a sharp knife and divide
　　the orange into sections, reserving any orange juice.
2) Line the serving plate with the shredded lettuce, arrange
　　the alfalfa sprouts in the centre.
3) Toss the banana in the lemon juice, add the cottage
　　cheese, orange segments and any orange juice, mix well.
4) Spoon the cottage cheese mixture around the alfalfa
　　sprouts. Sprinkle with the sunflower seeds and garnish
　　with the reserved orange zest.

Exchanges per serving:　1½ Fruit
　　　　　　　　　　　½ Vegetable
　　　　　　　　　　　1 Protein
　　　　　　　　　　　20 Optional Calories

Fruity Carrot Salad

Serves 2 **165 Calories per serving**

8oz (240g) carrots, grated
4oz (120g) canned crushed pineapple,
  no sugar added
1oz (30g) sultanas
1 tablespoon lemon juice
4 tablespoons low-fat
  natural yogurt
2 tablespoons low-calorie
  mayonnaise
salt and pepper to taste
2 teaspoons sesame seeds, toasted

1) Mix together the carrots, crushed pineapple and sultanas.
2) Place the lemon juice, yogurt, mayonnaise and seasoning in a jar, cover securely and shake vigorously.
3) Pour the dressing over the carrot mixture and toss well. Sprinkle with the toasted sesame seeds just before serving.

Exchanges per serving: 1½ Vegetable
1 Fruit
1½ Fat
40 Optional Calories

Marinated Carrot Salad

Serves 4 **65 Calories per serving**

4 tablespoons canned puréed
  (creamed) tomatoes
5 teaspoons white wine vinegar
4 teaspoons oil
¾ teaspoon Worcestershire sauce
¼ teaspoon salt
pinch mustard powder
9oz (270g) carrots, thinly sliced
½ small green pepper,
  seeded and chopped
1 stick celery, finely chopped
½ small onion, finely chopped

1) Blend the puréed tomatoes, vinegar oil, Worcestershire sauce, salt and mustard together in a small saucepan. Bring to the boil, reduce the heat and simmer gently for about 5 minutes stirring frequently. Leave to cool.
2) Mix the carrots, green pepper, celery and onion together in a bowl, pour over the tomato mixture and toss so all the vegetables are coated in the marinade.
3) Cover the salad and chill for at least 2 hours.

Exchanges per serving: 1½ Vegetable
1 Fat

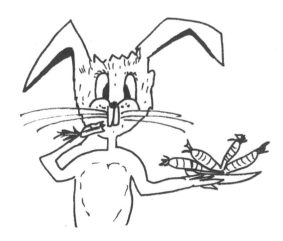

Spicy Pear Salad

Serves 2   **90 Calories per serving**

8oz (240g) drained canned pear
  halves with 4 tablespoons juice,
  no sugar added
2 tablespoons red wine vinegar
2″ (5cm) stick cinnamon
1 clove
2oz (60g) lettuce, shredded
4 teaspoons low-calorie mayonnaise
paprika

1) Place the pear juice, vinegar, cinnamon and clove in a
   small saucepan, bring to the boil and simmer until
   reduced to about 2-3 tablespoons.
2) Place the pear halves in a bowl and pour over the hot juice
   and spices, chill for several hours turning the fruit from
   time to time.
3) Line the two serving plates with the shredded lettuce,
   arrange the pear halves on top, strain the juice.
4) Stir the juice into the mayonnaise and spoon over the pear
   halves. Sprinkle with a little paprika and serve.

Exchanges per serving: 1 Fruit
                        $\frac{1}{2}$ Vegetable
                        1 Fat

Melon Salad

Serves 2   **75 Calories per serving**

1 medium apple, quartered,
  cored and chopped
1 tablespoon lemon juice
5oz (150g) melon, cut into chunks
  or scooped into balls
1$\frac{1}{2}$oz (45g) cucumber, finely chopped
2 sticks celery, chopped
4oz (120g) canned drained pineapple
  chunks with 2 tablespoons juice,
  no sugar added
1$\frac{1}{4}$ teaspoons chopped fresh chives
3 crisp lettuce leaves, shredded

1) Toss the apple in the lemon juice, add all the remaining
   ingredients except the lettuce and toss well.
2) Line a serving bowl with the shredded lettuce and pile the
   salad on top.

Exchanges per serving: 1$\frac{1}{2}$ Fruit
                        1 Vegetable

Courgette and Melon Salad

Serves 2   **150 Calories per serving**

8oz (240g) courgettes, sliced
salt
1½oz (45g) cucumber, chopped
2 spring onions, sliced
10oz (300g) melon, cut in chunks
   or scooped into balls
6oz (180g) tomatoes, quartered
3oz (90g) mushrooms, sliced
4 teaspoons vegetable oil
2 teaspoons lemon juice
pepper to taste

1) Cook the courgettes in boiling salted water for
   4-5 minutes, drain and cool.
2) Mix together the courgettes, cucumber, spring onions,
   melon, tomatoes and mushrooms.
3) Place the oil and lemon juice in a small jar, season with
   salt and pepper, cover securely and shake vigorously.
4) Pour the dressing over the salad and toss well.

Exchanges per serving: 1 Fruit
                           3½ Vegetable
                           2 Fat

Mushroom Salad

Serves 2   **155 Calories per serving**

2 x 1oz (30g) lean back bacon
8oz (240g) spinach, torn or
   roughly chopped
4oz (120g) mushrooms,
   thinly sliced
¼ teaspoon coriander seeds
2 teaspoons vegetable oil
2 teaspoons wine or cider vinegar
½ teaspoon lemon juice
salt and pepper to taste

1) Grill the bacon until crisp, leave to cool then crumble into
   small peices.
2) Mix together the spinach and sliced mushrooms.
3) Crush the coriander seeds in a pestle and mortar or with
   the end of a rolling pin against the side of a small basin.
   Whisk in the oil, vinegar, lemon juice and seasoning.
4) Pour the dressing over the spinach and mushrooms, toss
   well and transfer to the serving bowl. Top with the
   crumbled bacon.

Exchanges per serving: 2 Vegetable
                           1 Fat
                   100 Optional Calories

Rice Salad

Serves 2   **285 Calories per serving**

6oz (180g) cooked long grain rice
4 sticks celery, chopped
2 hard boiled eggs, chopped
¼ medium cucumber, chopped
1 medium onion, chopped
4 radishes, sliced
3 tablespoons low-fat natural yogurt
2 tablespoons low-calorie mayonnaise
2 teaspoons tomato relish
1 teaspoon Dijon-style mustard
salt and pepper to taste

1) Mix together the rice, celery, eggs, cucumber, onion and radishes.

2) Place the remaining ingredients in a small jar, cover securely and shake vigorously.

3) Pour the dressing over the rice salad and toss well. Cover and chill for at least 1 hour. Toss again before serving.

Exchanges per serving: 1 Bread
                       1 Protein
                       1½ Vegetable
                       1½ Fat
                       25 Optional Calories

Beetroot and Orange Salad

Serves 2   **100 Calories per serving**

6oz (180g) cooked beetroot
1 medium orange
2 teaspoons olive or vegetable oil
1 tablespoon lemon juice
salt and pepper to taste
sprigs of watercress

1) Remove the skin from the beetroot and slice thinly.

2) Using a sharp knife remove the peel and pith from the orange, slice thinly, catch any juices which may escape.

3) Place the oil and lemon juice and any reserved juices from slicing the orange in a jar, cover securely and shake vigorously.

4) Arrange the orange and beetroot slices alternately on a serving plate, pour over the dressing and garnish with the sprigs of watercress.

Exchanges per serving: 1 Vegetable
                       ½ Fruit
                       1 Fat

Minted Potato Salad

Serves 2 **145 Calories per serving**

6oz (180g) cooked potatoes, diced
3oz (90g) drained, canned sweetcorn
4 spring onions, chopped
4 teaspoons low-calorie
   mayonnaise
1 teaspoon lemon juice
1½ teaspoons chopped fresh mint
sprig of mint

1) Mix together the potatoes, sweetcorn and spring onions.
2) Stir the mayonnaise, lemon juice and mint together, add to the vegetables and mix well.
3) Transfer the salad to serving bowl and garnish with the sprig of mint.

Exchanges per serving: 1½ Bread
                       ½ Vegetable
                       1 Fat

Summer Salad

Serves 1 **75 Calories per serving**

2½fl oz (75ml) low-fat natural yogurt
1oz (30g) carrot, grated
2 spring onions, finely chopped
1 teaspoon chopped fresh dill or
   ½ teaspoon dried dill
1 small clove garlic, finely chopped
pinch each of salt and pepper
1 stick celery, finely chopped
3oz (90g) green beans, blanched
   and chopped
1 medium tomato, chopped
lettuce leaves

1) Mix the first six ingredients together in a bowl.
2) Add the celery, beans and tomato and mix well.
3) Arrange the lettuce leaves on serving plate and pile the mixture into centre.

Exchanges per serving: ½ Milk
                       4 Vegetable

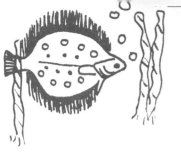

Fish

Prawn Cocktail

Serves 2 **115 Calories per serving**

½ small lettuce, shredded
4oz (120g) peeled prawns
2 tablespoons low-calorie mayonnaise
1 tablespoon lemon juice
1 tablespoon tomato purée
1 teaspoon Worcestershire sauce
2 slices of lemon

1) Divide the shredded lettuce between two serving dishes or glasses. Pile the prawns on top of the lettuce.

2) Stir the remaining ingredients together, mix well.

3) Spoon the sauce over the prawns and chill. Before serving cut from the centre of each lemon slice to the edge and twist each slice and arrange on top of the prawn cocktails.

Exchanges per serving: 2 Protein
½ Vegetable
1½ Fat
5 Optional Calories

Prawn and Sweetcorn Sauté

Serves 2 **260 Calories per serving**

1 teaspoon margarine
1 teaspoon vegetable oil
1 garlic clove, finely chopped
2oz (60g) spring onions, sliced
½ small red pepper, seeded and chopped
6oz (180g) drained, canned sweetcorn
½ teaspoon brown sugar
¼ teaspoon salt
pinch ground pepper
8oz (240g) peeled prawns
4 tablespoons water
1 teaspoon cornflour

1) Heat the margarine and oil in a frying pan. Add the garlic, spring onions and red pepper, sauté 3-4 minutes.

2) Mix in the sweetcorn, sugar, salt and pepper and stir over a medium heat until heated through. Add the prawns and sauté for a further 1-2 minutes.

3) Gradually blend the water into the cornflour to form a smooth paste, stir into the prawn mixture and cook for a further 1-2 minutes stirring all the time.

Exchanges per serving: 1 Fat
½ Vegetable
1 Bread
4 Protein
10 Optional Calories

Prawn Fritters

Serves 2　　　　　**315 Calories per serving**

2oz (60g) plain flour
pinch salt
6 tablespoons skimmed milk
1 egg
7oz (210g) peeled prawns, finely chopped
3 spring onions, finely chopped
2 teaspoons vegetable oil

1) Sift the flour and salt into a bowl. Mix together the milk and egg. Gradually beat into the flour to form a smooth batter.

2) Stir the prawns and onions into the batter and mix well.

3) Heat $\frac{1}{2}$-1 teaspoon oil in a non-stick frying pan. Drop one tablespoon of the prawn batter into the pan at a time. Cook until the underside is golden brown, turn and cook the other side. Repeat to use up all the batter adding the remaining oil as necessary. Serve warm.

Exchanges per serving:　1 Bread
　　　　　　　　　　　4 Protein
　　　　　　　　　　　$\frac{1}{4}$ Vegetable
　　　　　　　　　　　1 Fat
　　　　　　　　　　　15 Optional Calories

Simple Prawn Chow Mein

Serves 1　　　　　**195 Calories per serving**

2 sticks celery, finely chopped
4fl oz (120ml) chicken stock,
　made with $\frac{1}{2}$ a stock cube
1 small onion, chopped
1 tablespoon soy sauce
3oz (90g) drained canned bamboo
　shoots, chopped
3oz (90g) bean sprouts
4oz (120g) peeled prawns
$\frac{1}{4}$ teaspoon vegetable oil
3oz (90g) mushrooms, sliced

1) Place half the celery and all of the stock in a blender, blend until smooth, pour into a saucepan.

2) Stir the remaining celery, onion, soy sauce, bamboo shoots and bean sprouts into the saucepan. Bring to the boil, reduce the heat and simmer for 10 minutes. Stir in the prawns.

3) Heat the oil in a small non-stick frying pan, sauté the mushrooms until lightly browned.

4) Stir the mushrooms into the prawn mixture and serve.

Exchanges per serving:　4 Vegetable
　　　　　　　　　　　4 Protein
　　　　　　　　　　　$\frac{1}{2}$ Fat

31

Crabmeat Mousse

Serves 1   **280 Calories per serving**

4oz (120g) cooked white crabmeat
    or crab sticks
6 tablespoons tomato juice
1 tablespoon low-calorie mayonnaise
$\frac{1}{2}$oz (15g) drained canned
    pimientos, chopped
1 teaspoon lemon juice
$\frac{1}{2}$ teaspoon chopped fresh parsley
1$\frac{1}{2}$ teaspoons chopped fresh chives
9 tablespoons water, divided
1 tablespoon gelatine
salt and pepper to taste
$\frac{1}{2}$oz (15g) low-fat dry milk

1) Flake the crabmeat into a bowl, add 1 tablespoon tomato
juice, the mayonnaise, pimientos, lemon juice, parsley
and 1 teaspoon chives, mix well.
2) Measure 4 tablespoons water into a cup or small bowl,
sprinkle in the gelatine stirring all the time. Stand the cup
in a saucepan of simmering water and leave until the
gelatine has completely dissolved. Stir into the crabmeat
mixture. Season with salt and pepper.
3) Mix the low-fat dry milk with the remaining water, fold
into the crab mixture. Transfer to a small mould. Chill
well until set.
4) To serve, dip the mould in hot water and turn the mousse
out onto a serving plate. Spoon the remaining tomato
juice round the mousse and sprinkle with the remaining
chopped chives.

Exchanges per serving: 4 Protein
                      1$\frac{1}{2}$ Fat
                      $\frac{1}{2}$ Milk
                      10 Optional Calories

Prawn Stuffed Plaice

Serves 2   **265 Calories per serving**

2 x 4oz (120g) plaice fillets
salt and pepper to taste
4oz (120g) peeled prawns
3 teaspoons margarine
2 teaspoons plain flour
$\frac{1}{4}$ pint (150ml) skimmed milk
1 teaspoon chopped fresh chives

1) Lay the plaice fillets out skin side uppermost and season
with salt and pepper.
2) Roughly chop and reserve 1oz (30g) prawns, divide the
remainder between the two fillets and roll the plaice
around them, secure each roll with a cocktail stick.
3) Place in a small ovenproof dish and dot with 1 teaspoon
margarine. Cover and bake at 375F/190C/Gas 5 for
15-20 minutes.
4) Melt the remaining 2 teaspoons margarine in a small
saucepan, stir in the flour and stir over a low heat for
30 seconds. Gradually blend in the milk and bring to the
boil, stirring all the time. Add the reserved prawns and
chives and simmer for 1-2 minutes stirring constantly.
5) Transfer the plaice to a warm serving plate, remove the
cocktail sticks and pour over the prawn and chive sauce.

Exchanges per serving: 4 Protein
                      1$\frac{1}{2}$ Fat
                      $\frac{1}{4}$ Milk
                      10 Optional Calories

Tuna Pancake Rolls

Serves 2 **390 Calories per serving**

2oz (60g) plain flour
1 egg
6 tablespoons skimmed milk
1 teaspoon vegetable oil
6oz (180g) drained canned tuna, flaked
6oz (180g) drained canned sweetcorn
3oz (90g) bean sprouts, roughly chopped
½ teaspoon dried oregano
1 teaspoon chopped fresh chives
salt and pepper to taste

1) Sieve the flour into a bowl. Mix together the egg and milk, gradually beat into the flour to form a smooth batter.

2) Heat ¼ teaspoon oil in a small non-stick frying pan. Spoon a quarter of the batter into the pan, swirl round and cook until the underside begins to brown, turn and cook the other side. Repeat until all the oil and batter has been used to make four small pancakes.

3) Mix the tuna, sweetcorn, bean sprouts, oregano and chives together in a bowl. Season well with salt and pepper.

4) Place a quarter of the tuna mixture in the centre of each pancake, form into a roll shape and folding over the pancake to make an envelope shape.

5) Transfer the pancake rolls to an ovenproof dish, make sure the pancake roll folds are underneath each roll. Cover with foil and bake at 400F/200C/Gas 6 for 10 minutes. Remove the foil and continue baking for a further 5 minutes until crisp.

Exchanges per serving: 2 Bread
3½ Protein
½ Vegetable
½ Fat
15 Optional Calories

Cod in a Parcel

Serves 2 **130 Calories per serving**

10oz (300g) cod fillet
3 tablespoons chopped fresh dill
2 tablespoons chopped spring onions
3 tablespoons soy sauce
½ clove garlic, crushed
½ teaspoon Worcestershire sauce
pepper to taste
2 sprigs of dill

1) Cut a piece of baking parchment large enough to enclose the cod, lay it on a baking sheet.

2) Sprinkle half the dill and spring onions over the centre of the parchment, lay the cod fillet on top.

3) Mix together the soy sauce, garlic, Worcestershire sauce and pepper in a small bowl. Pour the mixture over the cod and sprinkle with the remaining dill and spring onions.

4) Fold over the parchment to completely enclose the fillet and bake at 350F/180C/Gas 4 for 20-25 minutes.

5) Carefully unwrap the parchment and check the fish is cooked, it should flake easily when tested with a fork. Cut the cod fillet in half and transfer to a warm serving plate. Garnish with the sprigs of dill.

Exchanges per serving: 4 Protein
¼ Vegetable

Baked Red Mullet

Serves 2   310 Calories per serving

4 teaspoons margarine
1 garlic clove, crushed
6oz (180g) courgettes, sliced
1 medium onion, sliced and
    separated into rings
½ red pepper, seeded and sliced
½ green pepper, seeded and sliced
3oz (90g) mushrooms, sliced
2 x 8oz (240g) red mullet
salt and pepper to taste

1) Melt the margarine in a small pan. Add the garlic and
   vegetables and sauté for 5 minutes.
2) Cut two squares of foil large enough to wrap each fish in.
   Place the red mullet in the centre of each piece of foil,
   arrange the vegetables around each fish.
3) Sprinkle the red mullet and vegetables with salt and
   pepper and fold over the foil to securely enclose the fish.
4) Bake in oven at 375F/190C/Gas 5 for 30 minutes.

Exchanges per serving: 2 Fat
                        2½ Vegetable
                        5 Protein

Skate with Lemon Sauce

Serves 2   170 Calories per serving

12fl oz (360ml) water
1 stick celery, including leaves
1 bouquet garni
3 tablespoons plus 1 teaspoon wine vinegar
½ teaspoon salt
6 peppercorns
few fish trimmings if available
2 x 5oz (150g) wings of skate
1 teaspoon vegetable oil
1 large onion, sliced and separated into rings
juice and grated zest of 1 lemon
1 teaspoon chopped fresh parsley
1 teaspoon chopped fresh thyme
salt and pepper to taste
2 teaspoons cornflour, blended
    with 1 tablespoon water
4 sprigs of watercress

1) Prepare a court bouillon by placing ½ pint (300ml) water in
   a saucepan with the celery, bouquet garni, 3 tablespoons
   wine vinegar, salt, peppercorns and fish trimmings if
   available in a saucepan. Bring to the boil, reduce the heat
   and simmer gently for 25-30 minutes. Leave to cool.
2) Cut each wing in half and place in a large saucepan,
   strain the court bouillon over the fish. Gradually bring to
   simmering point over a low heat. Simmer for 10 minutes.
3) Heat the oil in a separate non-stick saucepan, add the
   onion and sauté until transparent. Stir in the lemon juice,
   remaining water and vinegar, chopped parsley and
   thyme. Bring to the boil, stir in the cornflour paste and
   lemon zest. Simmer 1-2 minutes, stirring all the time,
   until the sauce has thickened.
4) Transfer the skate to a warm serving plate, pour over the
   lemon sauce and garnish with the sprigs of watercress.

Exchanges per serving: ½ Fat
                        1 Vegetable
                        4 Protein
                        10 Optional Calories

Mackerel Grill

Serves 2   **335 Calories per serving**

2 x 7oz mackerel, cleaned
1 tablespoon vegetable oil
2 tablespoons lemon juice
$\frac{1}{4}$ teaspoon salt
$\frac{1}{2}$ teaspoon caraway seeds
$\frac{1}{2}$ lemon, cut into wedges

1) Make three diagonal cuts approximately $\frac{1}{4}''$ (5mm) deep through the skin on each side of the mackerel.

2) Brush each fish all over with the oil and lemon juice and sprinkle one side with salt and a few caraway seeds, reserving half for the other side of the mackerel.

3) Place the fish on the rack of the grill pan and grill under a preheated grill for about 7-8 minutes.

4) Turn the mackerel over and sprinkle with the reserved salt and caraway seeds. Return to the grill and cook for a further 7-8 minutes. You will be able to tell when fish is cooked as the eyes will have turned white in colour and the flesh will flake easily.

5) Transfer the mackerel to warm serving plates and garnish with the lemon wedges.

Exchanges per serving: 5 Protein
                        1½ Fat
                        5 Optional Calories

Fish Fillets Banane

Serves 2   **225 Calories per serving**

1 tablespoon margarine, divided
1 medium banana, sliced thickly
2 x 5oz (150g) cod or haddock fillets
2 teaspoons seasoned flour
1 teaspoon lemon juice
1 teaspoon chopped fresh parsley
2 lemon wedges

1) Heat 1 teaspoon margarine in a medium size frying pan, add the banana slices and sauté until golden, remove from the pan.

2) Turn the cod or haddock fillets in the seasoned flour.

3) Heat the remaining margarine in the same frying pan. Add the fish fillets and cook until the underside is golden brown, turn and brown the other side. To check the fish is cooked test by flaking the fish with a fork.

4) Transfer the fish to a warm serving plate and keep warm.

5) Stir the lemon juice into the juices in the frying pan, add sautéed banana slices and cook over a low heat until heated through, sprinkle over the fish and top with the chopped parsley. Serve with the lemon wedges.

Exchanges per serving: 1½ Fat
                        1 Fruit
                        4 Protein
                        10 Optional Calories

Grilled Turbot with Tartare Sauce

Serves 2 **215 Calories per serving**

2 x 8oz (240g) turbot steaks
2 tablespoons lemon juice
salt and pepper to taste
2 tablespoons low-calorie mayonnaise
1 tablespoon lemon juice
1 tablespoon drained chopped capers
2 small gherkins, finely chopped
2 lemon wedges

1) Place the turbot steaks on a sheet of foil laying on the rack of the grill pan. Brush with half the lemon juice and sprinkle with salt and pepper.

2) Grill the steaks for about 5 minutes under a preheated grill, turn, brush with the remaining lemon juice and sprinkle with salt and pepper. Return to the grill for a further 5 minutes or until the fish flakes easily when tested with a fork.

3) Meanwhile combine the mayonnaise, lemon juice, capers and gherkins, mix well.

4) Place the turbot steaks on a warm serving plate, garnish with the lemon wedges and serve the tartare sauce separately.

Exchanges per serving: 5 Protein
1½ Fat

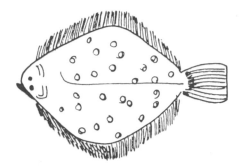

Peppered Cod

Serves 1 **185 Calories per serving**

1 medium red pepper
1 medium green pepper
1 small onion, finely chopped
2 tablespoons tomato puree
6 tablespoons water
salt and pepper to taste
5oz (150g) skinned cod fillet
  cut into 1½" (3.75 cm) cubes

1) Place the peppers on the rack of the grill pan and grill under a preheated grill, turning frequently until black and blistered. Plunge into a bowl of cold water.

2) Stir the onion, tomato puree and water together, season with salt and pepper and pour into a shallow flameproof dish. Add the cod and bring to the boil over a low heat, cover and simmer for about 12 minutes.

3) While the fish is cooking; skin, core and seed the peppers, cut into thin strips.

4) Arrange the strips of pepper over the fish cover and simmer for a further 3-4 minutes to heat through.

Exchanges per serving: 3 Vegetable
4 Protein
20 Optional Calories

Stuffed Trout

Serves 1　　　　　　　　**300 Calories per serving**

1 teaspoon vegetable oil
1 small onion, chopped
½ clove garlic, finely chopped
½ medium green pepper,
　seeded and chopped
1 medium tomato, blanched,
　peeled and chopped
1½ teaspoons chopped fresh parsley
1 teaspoon lemon juice
¼ teaspoon salt
dash pepper
1 x 8oz (240g) whole trout, cleaned
2 lemon slices

1) Heat the oil in a non-stick frying pan. Sauté the onion and garlic until transparent. Add the green pepper and sauté for a further 2 minutes.

2) Stir the tomato, parsley, lemon juice, salt and pepper into the onion mixture, mix well.

3) Spoon the stuffing into the trout and transfer to an ovenproof dish; pour any accumulated liquid over the fish. Bake at 350F/180C/Gas 4 for approximately 25 minutes. You will be able to tell when the fish is cooked as the eyes will have turned white in colour and the flesh will flake easily.

5) Transfer the trout to a serving plate and serve with the lemon slices.

Exchanges per serving:　1 Fat
　　　　　　　　　　　2 Vegetable
　　　　　　　　　　　5 Protein

Skate Toledo

Serves 2　　　　　　　　**360 Calories per serving**

1 teaspoon margarine
1 small clove garlic, finely chopped, optional
1 small onion, sliced and separated into rings
½ medium green pepper, seeded and thinly sliced
2oz (60g) long grain rice
6fl oz (180ml) chicken stock,
　made with ½ a stock cube
2 medium tomatoes, blanched, skinned and chopped
salt and pepper to taste
12oz (360g) skate wings
4 teaspoons seasoned flour
2 teaspoons vegetable oil
1 teaspoon chopped fresh parsley

1) Melt the margarine in a non-stick saucepan. Sauté the garlic, onion and green pepper 1-2 minutes.

2) Stir in the rice and stock, cover and simmer gently for 10 minutes. Stir in the tomatoes and seasoning, cover and continue cooking until all the liquid has been absorbed and the rice cooked.

3) Meanwhile prepare the skate: Cut each wing into two or three pieces, turn in the seasoned flour.

4) Heat the oil in a frying pan, add the skate and cook until the underside is golden, 3-4 minutes, turn and cook the other side.

5) Spread rice over a warmed serving plate, arrange the skate wings on top and sprinkle with the chopped parsley.

Exchanges per serving:　1½ Fat
　　　　　　　　　　　1½ Vegetable
　　　　　　　　　　　1 Bread
　　　　　　　　　　　4 Protein
　　　　　　　　　　　20 Optional Calories

Whiting with Mustard Sauce

Serves 1　　　　　　　**185 Calories per serving**

5oz (150g) whiting fillet
1 medium onion, chopped
1 tablespoon French mustard
4 tablespoons wine vinegar
juice of $\frac{1}{2}$ a lemon
1 tablespoon chopped fresh parsley
salt and pepper to taste

1) Lay the whiting in an ovenproof dish. Sprinkle over the onions.
2) Blend the mustard and vinegar together, pour over the fish cover and bake at 350F/180C/Gas 4 for about 20 minutes or until the fish flakes easily with a fork.
3) Transfer the whiting to a serving plate and keep warm. Pour the cooking liquid into a saucepan, stir in the lemon juice and boil briskly for 3-4 minutes stirring all the time to reduce the liquid. Stir in the parsley, season to taste and pour over the fish.

Exchanges per serving:　4 Protein
　　　　　　　　　　　　1 Vegetable

Haddock with Egg and Dill Sauce

Serves 2　　　　　　　**230 Calories per serving**

9oz (270g) haddock fillet
$\frac{1}{4}$ pint (150ml) skimmed milk
2 teaspoons chopped fresh dill
salt and pepper to taste
2 teaspoons margarine
1 tablespoon plain flour
1 hard boiled egg, chopped

1) Divide the haddock into two, place in a saucepan and cover with the milk. Add the dill and seasoning, cover and simmer gently for 8-10 minutes.
2) Drain and reserve the milk, keep the haddock warm.
3) Melt the margarine in a small saucepan, stir in the flour and gradually blend in the warm milk.
4) Bring to the boil, stirring all the time, boil 1-2 minutes until thickened. Add the chopped egg and adjust the seasoning. Pour the egg and dill sauce over the haddock and serve.

Exchanges per serving:　4 Protein
　　　　　　　　　　　　$\frac{1}{4}$ Milk
　　　　　　　　　　　　1 Fat
　　　　　　　　　　　　15 Optional Calories

Monkfish Kebabs

Serves 2   **180 Calories per serving**

10oz (300g) monkfish
1 small green pepper, seeded
    and cut into 1″ (2.5cm) cubes
8oz (240g) pickling onions or shallots
2 medium tomatoes, halved
8 button mushrooms
4 bay leaves
2 tablespoons lemon juice
1 teaspoon vegetable oil
salt and pepper to taste
¼ teaspoon paprika

1) Cut the monkfish into 1″ (2.5cm) cubes.

2) Blanch the green pepper and onions in boiling water for
    1½-2 minutes. Drain.

3) Thread the fish, vegetables and bay leaves alternately on
    to skewers.

4) Mix the lemon juice, oil, salt and pepper together. Brush
    over the kebabs and place under a preheated grill for 8-10
    minutes brushing with more lemon juice and turning
    every 2-3 minutes.

5) Transfer to a serving plate, sprinkle with paprika and
    serve with a crisp green salad.

Exchanges per serving: 4 Protein
                        3 Vegetable

Cheesy Fish Grill

Serves 1   **265 Calories per serving**

1 slice (1oz/30g) bread
2oz (60g) cooked smoked fish
1 small onion, finely sliced
1 medium tomato, sliced
salt and pepper to taste
1oz (30g) Cheddar cheese, grated

1) Toast the bread on one side.

2) Lay the fish on the untoasted side, cover with the slices of
    onion. Top with the tomato. Sprinkle with salt and pepper
    and the grated cheese.

3) Grill under a moderate heat to allow the fish to heat
    through and the cheese to melt and brown.

Exchanges per serving: 1 Bread
                        3 Protein
                        1½ Vegetable

Mackerel in Yogurt

Serves 2   **325 Calories per serving**

6oz (180g) cucumber, thinly sliced
3 tablespoons wine vinegar
2 x 6oz (180g) mackerel
1 teaspoon dried mixed herbs
¼ teaspoon salt
¼ teaspoon pepper
10fl oz (300ml) low-fat
  natural yogurt
1 small onion, thinly sliced
  and separated into rings
1 teaspoon chopped parsley
sprinkle of paprika

1) Cut each slice of cucumber into quarters, cover with the vinegar and leave to marinade for 2 hours.
2) Sprinkle the mackerel, inside and out, with the herbs, salt and pepper. Place under a hot grill for 10-12 minutes, turning once. Leave to cool. Remove the skin and bones and flake the fish.
3) Season the yogurt with salt and pepper.
4) Arrange layers of onion, cucumber, yogurt and mackerel alternately in a serving bowl. Reserve a few slices of cucumber but continue with the layers until all the ingredients are used up ending with a layer of yogurt.
5) Sprinkle the yogurt with the chopped parsley and paprika. Arrange the cucumber slices around the edge of the bowl.

Exchanges per serving: 4 Protein
                        1½ Vegetable
                        1 Milk

Simple Fish Bake

Serves 2   **130 Calories per serving**

5oz (150g) white fish fillet
  e.g. cod, haddock, coley
1-2 teaspoons lemon juice
4oz (120g) peeled prawns
2 teaspoons chopped fresh chives
2 teaspoons chopped fresh parsley
salt and pepper to taste
2 medium tomatoes, sliced
2 tablespoons skimmed milk

1) Line a small ovenproof dish with foil leaving sufficient laying over the edge to cover the dish. Lay the fish in the lined dish and sprinkle with lemon juice.
2) Arrange the prawns over the fish fillet and sprinkle the herbs, salt and pepper over the top.
3) Place the tomato slices round the edge of the dish.
4) Pour the milk over the fish. Draw the foil over to cover the ingredients and bake at 375F/190C/Gas 5 for 20 minutes.

Exchanges per serving: 4 Protein
                        1 Vegetable
                        5 Optional Calories

South American Fish

Serves 2   **180 Calories per serving**

1 teaspoon vegetable oil
1 small onion, thinly sliced
½ medium green pepper, seeded and sliced
1 stick celery, chopped
1 small carrot, chopped
1 small clove garlic, crushed
14oz (420g) can tomatoes, chopped
6 tablespoons canned, puréed
   (creamed) tomatoes
4fl oz (120ml) chicken or vegetable
   stock made with ½ a stock cube
¼ teaspoon dried basil
¼ teaspoon dried oregano
dash hot pepper sauce
10oz (300g) boneless fish e.g. monkfish,
   halibut or cod, cut into 1″ (2.5cm) pieces

1) Heat the oil in a saucepan, add the onion, green pepper,
   celery, carrot and garlic, sauté for 2 minutes.
2) Stir in the remaining ingredients, except the fish. Bring to
   the boil, reduce the heat and simmer for about 20 minutes.
3) Stir in the fish and simmer for a further 6-10 minutes until
   the fish flakes easily when tested with a fork.

Exchanges per serving: ½ Fat
                      4 Vegetable
                      4 Protein

Fishermans Flan

Serves 4   **370 Calories per serving**

3oz (90g) plain flour
pinch salt
8 teaspoons margarine
4 tablespoons low-fat natural yogurt
9oz (270g) cooked smoked skinless
   haddock fillet, flaked
6oz (180g) drained canned sweetcorn
2 x 1oz (30g) lean back bacon, grilled and chopped
2 eggs
½ pint (300ml) skimmed milk
sprinkling of pepper
sprigs of watercress

1) Sieve the flour and salt into a bowl. Rub in the margarine
   until the mixture resembles fine breadcrumbs. Mix in the
   yogurt to form a dough, cover and chill for at least 1 hour.
2) Roll out the pastry between two sheets of baking
   parchment, line a 7″ (17.5cm) flan tin.
3) Spread the haddock and sweetcorn over the base of the
   flan case. Sprinkle over the chopped bacon.
4) Beat the eggs, milk and pepper together, pour into the
   flan. Bake at 375F/190C/Gas 5 for 30 minutes until
   golden and firm to touch. Serve hot or cold garnished with
   the sprigs of watercress.

Exchanges per serving: 1 Bread
                      2 Fat
                      2½ Protein
                      ¼ Milk
                      100 Optional Calories

Smoked Haddock in Cheesy Corn Sauce

Serves 2   **340 Calories per serving**

5oz (150g) smoked haddock fillet
¼ pint (150ml) skimmed milk
2 teaspoons margarine
2 teaspoons plain flour
salt and pepper to taste
6oz (180g) drained canned sweetcorn
2oz (60g) Cheddar cheese, grated
2 teaspoons chopped fresh chives
1 medium tomato, sliced

1) Poach the haddock in the milk for 3-4 minutes or until it flakes easily when tested with a fork. Leave to cool, remove the skin and any bones, flake the fish and reserve the milk.

2) Melt the margarine in a small saucepan, add the flour and stir well, gradually blend in the reserved milk. Bring to the boil stirring all the time, simmer for 1 minute, season with salt and pepper and stir in half the cheese.

3) Spread the sweetcorn over the base of an ovenproof dish, cover with the flaked haddock. Pour over the cheese sauce, sprinkle with the chives and remaining cheese.

4) Grill under a low heat for about 10 minutes to allow the sweetcorn and fish to heat through. Arrange the tomato slices on top and grill for a further minute.

Exchanges per serving: 3 Protein
            1 Bread
            ¼ Milk
            1 Fat
            ½ Vegetable
          10 Optional Calories

Salmon Loaf

Serves 4   **220 Calories per serving**

15oz (450g) drained canned salmon, flaked
6oz (180g) drained canned
   water chestnuts, chopped
1 egg, beaten
2 sticks celery, finely chopped
1 small onion, chopped
6 tablespoons tomato purée
1 teaspoon chopped fresh dill
¼ teaspoon Worcestershire sauce
dash of hot pepper sauce
4 lime or lemon wedges
2 sprigs of dill

1) Lay a piece of baking parchment on a baking sheet.

2) In a large bowl mix together all the ingredients except the lime or lemon wedges and sprigs of dill.

3) Transfer the salmon mixture to the baking parchment and shape into a loaf shape.

4) Bake at 350F/180C/Gas 4 for 35-45 minutes until lightly browned. Allow to stand for at least 15 minutes and serve warm or cool or cover and refrigerate for up to 3 days.

5) Slice the loaf and serve garnished with the lime or lemon wedges and sprigs of dill.

Exchanges per serving: 4 Protein
            ½ Bread
            ½ Vegetable
          15 Optional Calories

Mackerel Dolmades

Serves 2   **225 Calories per serving**

4 large cabbage leaves
8oz (240g) canned mackerel
    steaks, drained
½ small red pepper, seeded
    and chopped
2 teaspoons tomato purée
½ teaspoon grated lemon zest
1 teaspoon chopped fresh basil
    or ½ teaspoon dried basil
salt and pepper to taste
¼ pint (150ml) chicken stock,
    made with ½ stock cube
2 teaspoons cornflour
4 lemon wedges
2 sprigs of fresh basil

1) Boil the whole cabbage leaves in water for a few minutes
    until soft, drain well.

2) Mash the mackerel steaks in a bowl. Add the red pepper,
    tomato purée, lemon zest, basil, salt and pepper, mix well.

3) Divide the mackerel mixture between the four cabbage
    leaves. Fold the leaves over to enclose the filling, carefully
    transfer to an ovenproof dish.

4) Pour stock over the dolmades, cover and cook in a
    preheated oven at 325F/170C/Gas 3 for 35 minutes.

5) Drain off the stock and gradually blend into the cornflour.
    Pour into a small saucepan and bring to the boil, stirring
    all the time. Simmer for a minute.

6) Transfer the dolmades to serving plates, pour over the
    thickened stock and garnish with the lemon wedges and
    sprigs of basil.

Exchanges per serving: 4 Protein
                        2 Vegetable
                        15 Optional Calories

Tuna and Pear Bake

Serves 2   **225 Calories per serving**

2 canned pear halves with
    2 tablespoons juice
6oz (180g) drained canned
    tuna, flaked
1 stick celery, chopped
½ green pepper, seeded
    and chopped
1 small onion, chopped
1 teaspoon grated lemon zest
8 teaspoons low-calorie mayonnaise
¼ teaspoon curry powder
salt and pepper to taste
4 sprigs of watercress

1) Cut four thin slices from the pear, put to one side.

2) Chop the remaining pear, mix in the pear juice, tuna,
    celery, green pepper, onion and lemon zest.

3) Mix the mayonnaise and curry powder together, stir into
    the tuna mixture, season with salt and pepper.

4) Transfer the tuna mixture to a small ovenproof dish, top
    with the reserved pear slices and bake 350F/180C/Gas 4
    for about 20 minutes until slightly browned. Serve
    garnished with watercress.

Exchanges per serving: ½ Fruit
                        3 Protein
                        1 Vegetable
                        2 Fat

Cheese and Prawn Baked Potatoes

Serves 2   285 Calories per serving

4oz (120g) low-fat soft cheese
1 small clove garlic, crushed
2 teaspoons chopped fresh chives
4oz (120g) peeled prawns
salt and pepper to taste
2 x 6oz (180g) hot baked potatoes

1) Mash the soft cheese, garlic and chives together in a small bowl, stir in half the prawns and season with salt and pepper.
2) Cut three quarters of the way through the length of each potato and open out. Divide the cheese mixture between the two potatoes.
3) Decorate with the remaining prawns and serve immediately.

Exchanges per serving: 3 Protein
                               2 Bread

Simple Kipper Pâté

Serves 2   170 Calories per serving

5oz (150g) kipper, head removed
4oz (120g) low-fat soft cheese
3 tablespoons low-fat
    natural yogurt
juice of $\frac{1}{2}$ a lemon
1oz (30g) gherkins, chopped
1 tablespoon chopped fresh parsley
black pepper to taste
3 lemon slices
sprig of parsley

1) Grill or poach the kipper until cooked, the flesh should flake easily when tested with a fork. Leave until cool, remove the skin and as many bones as possible. Flake the flesh.
2) Mash the cheese and yogurt together. Gradually add the flaked fish, lemon juice, gherkins, chopped parsley and pepper or place all the ingredients in a blender and blend until smooth.
3) Transfer the pâté to a small dish, roughen the top with a fork and garnish with the slices of lemon and sprig of parsley.

Exchanges per serving: 3 Protein
                               15 Optional Calories

Meat

Index

Lamb Chops Diable

Serves 2   **260 Calories per serving**

1 garlic clove, crushed
½ teaspoon dried oregano
2 tablespoons lemon juice
1 teaspoon Dijon-style mustard
1 teaspoon clear honey
12oz (360g) lamb loin chops –
　　about ½″ (1cm) thick
2 tablespoons dried breadcrumbs

1) Place the garlic, oregano, lemon juice, mustard and honey in a jar, cover securely and shake vigorously.

2) Lay the lamb chops on the rack of the grill pan, brush with half the garlic mixture and cook under a hot grill for 3-4 minutes.

3) Turn the chops over, brush with the remaining garlic mixture and grill for a further 3 minutes or according to taste.

4) Sprinkle the chops with the breadcrumbs and grill for a further 30 seconds until golden.

Exchanges per serving:　4 Protein
　　　　　　　　　　　　40 Optional Calories

Lamb Stew

Serves 2   **335 Calories per serving**

10oz (300g) lean lamb fillet
1 medium onion, sliced
1 stick celery, chopped, reserve the leaves
4oz (120g) carrots, sliced
4oz (120g) swede, chopped
6oz (180g) potatoes, chopped
½ teaspoon dried mixed herbs
salt and pepper to taste
¾ pint (450ml) chicken or vegetable
　　stock, made with ½ a stock cube

1) Trim all visible fat from the meat, place on the rack of a grill pan and cook turning once, under a hot grill until all the juices stop running.

2) Cut the meat into 1″ (2.5cm) cubes and place in a small saucepan with all the remaining ingredients, except the celery leaves.

3) Bring the stew to the boil, reduce the heat to low, cover and gently simmer for 30-40 minutes until the meat and vegetables are cooked.

4) Finely chop the celery leaves and sprinkle over each serving of stew.

Exchanges per serving:　4 Protein
　　　　　　　　　　　　2 Vegetable
　　　　　　　　　　　　1 Bread

Shepherds Pie

Serves 1   **350 Calories per serving**

4fl oz (120ml) tomato juice
4 tablespoons chicken or vegetable
    stock, made with ½ a stock cube
1 medium onion, chopped
1 medium carrot, chopped
½ teaspoon dried mixed herbs
4oz (120g) minced cooked lamb
3oz (90g) cooked potato, mashed
paprika

1) Place the tomato juice, stock, onion, carrot and herbs in a
   saucepan. Bring to boil, reduce the heat, cover and
   simmer for 15 minutes.
2) Add the cooked lamb and simmer for a further 5 minutes.
3) Spoon the meat mixture into a small deep ovenproof dish,
   spread the potato over the top and dust with a sprinkling
   of paprika.
4) Bake at 400F/200C/Gas 6 for 15 minutes or until turning
   brown.

Exchanges per serving: ½ Fruit
                         2 Vegetable
                         4 Protein
                         1 Bread

Lamb Lasagne

Serves 2   **515 Calories per serving**

1 teaspoon vegetable oil
1 clove garlic, finely chopped
1 medium onion, chopped
6oz (180g) cooked minced lamb
8oz (240g) can tomatoes
1 tablespoon tomato purée
½ vegetable stock cube, crumbled
1½oz (45g) uncooked lasagne
1 tablespoon margarine
½oz (15g) plain flour
¼ pint (150ml) skimmed milk
1oz (30g) Cheddar cheese, grated
1 egg, beaten
salt and pepper to taste

1) Heat the oil in a frying pan, sauté the garlic and onion for
   1-2 minutes, add the lamb, tomatoes, tomato purée and
   crumbled stock cube. Bring to the boil, stirring all the
   time reduce the heat and simmer 1-2 minutes.
2) Layer the lasagne and lamb mixture in an ovenproof dish.
3) Melt the margarine in a saucepan, stir in the flour and
   cook over a moderate heat for 1 minute. Gradually add
   the milk, Bring to the boil stirring all the time.
4) Remove from the heat and stir in ½oz (15g) cheese, the
   beaten egg and seasoning to taste. Stir until the cheese has
   melted then pour over the lasagne.
5) Sprinkle the top with the remaining cheese and bake at
   350F/180C/Gas 4 for 30-40 minutes until the lasagne is
   cooked and the top golden brown.

Exchanges per serving: 2 Fat
                         2 Vegetable
                         4 Protein
                         1 Bread
                         ¼ Milk
                         5 Optional Calories

Coriander Lamb Steaks

Serves 2   **245 Calories per serving**

1 tablespoon coriander seeds
1 clove garlic
¼ teaspoon salt
2 x 5oz (150g) lamb steaks, cut from
   the top of the leg
sprigs of mint

1) Crush the coriander seeds using a pestle and mortar or place in a small basin and press the seeds against the side of the basin with a rolling pin.

2) Mix together the coriander, garlic and salt. Press the mixture on to both sides of the lamb and leave in a cool place for at least 1 hour.

3) Lay the lamb steaks on the rack of a grill pan and cook under a hot grill for 12-15 minutes, turning once. Both sides of the steak should be crisp and brown. Serve on a warm plate garnished with sprigs of mint.

Exchanges per serving: 4 Protein

Persian Lamb

Serves 2   **365 Calories per serving**

2 cloves garlic, crushed
1 small onion, chopped
3 medium tomatoes, blanched
   skinned and roughly chopped
8oz (240g) cooked lamb, cut
   in 1″ (2.5cm) cubes
¼ teaspoon ground allspice
¼ teaspoon ground mace
¼ teaspoon ground coriander
¼ teaspoon ground ginger
¼ teaspoon pepper
¼ teaspoon salt
4fl oz (120ml) chicken or vegetable
   stock, made with ½ a cube
1 medium apple, peeled, quartered,
   cored and chopped
½ teaspoon powdered turmeric
6oz (180g) cooked long grain rice, hot
1 lemon, sliced

1) Place the garlic, onion, tomatoes and meat in a saucepan.

2) Stir in the spices and salt and mix well. Add the stock and bring to the boil. Reduce the heat and simmer gently for 10-15 minutes. Add the apple and cook for a further 3-4 minutes.

3) Stir the turmeric into the rice and mix well then spread round the edge of a warm serving plate. Pile the lamb mixture in the centre and decorate with the lemon slices.

Exchanges per serving: 2 Vegetable
                        4 Protein
                        ½ Fruit
                        1 Bread

Fruited Pork Chops

Serves 2   **405 Calories per serving**

2 x 6oz (180g) loin chops
1 medium carrot, thinly sliced
2fl oz (60ml) unsweetened apple juice
1 small onion, chopped
1 stick celery, chopped
½ medium mango, peeled, stoned,
   cut into ½" (1cm) pieces
½ medium apple, peeled, quartered,
   cored and chopped
½oz (15g) sultanas
6oz (180g) cooked long grain rice (hot)

1) Place the chops on the rack of the grill pan and cook under
   a preheated grill for about 6 minutes, turning once, set
   aside.
2) Mix together all the remaining ingredients except the
   rice, transfer to an ovenproof dish and lay the pork chops
   on top.
3) Cover the dish with foil and bake at 350F/180C/Gas 4 for
   35-45 minutes until the vegetables are cooked.
4) Divide the hot rice between two warm plates, top with the
   baked chops, fruit and vegetables.

Exchanges per serving: 4 Protein
                             1 Vegetable
                             1 Fruit
                             1 Bread

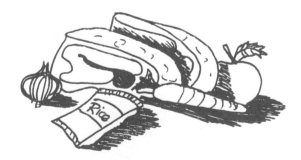

Sesame Pork

Serves 2   **295 Calories per serving**

10oz (300g) pork fillet
4fl oz (120ml) chicken stock made
   with ½ a stock cube
4 teaspoons soy sauce
2 teaspoons dry sherry
1 teaspoon clear honey
½ star anise or pinch of 5 spice powder
2 teaspoons vegetable oil
½ medium red pepper, seeded and
   cut into thin strips
2oz (60g) bean sprouts
1 teaspoon sesame seeds, toasted

1) Place pork in a shallow flat dish. Combine stock, soy
   sauce, sherry, honey and star anise or 5 spice powder
   and pour over fillet; cover dish and refrigerate for at least
   2 hours, turning the meat frequently in marinade.
2) Transfer pork to a rack in a baking dish, discarding star
   anise and reserving marinade. Bake at 325F/160C/Gas 3
   for 30 minutes. Remove meat from rack and slice.
3) Heat oil in a wok or frying pan. Add pork, pepper strips,
   bean sprouts and sesame seeds and stir-fry for 4 minutes.
   Add reserved marinade and cook, stirring occasionally
   until liquid is evaporated; divide evenly.

Exchanges per serving: 4 Protein
                             1 Fat
                             1 Vegetable
                             25 Optional Calories

Porkburgers

Serves 1 **230 Calories per serving**

5oz (150g) lean pork, minced
1 small onion, finely chopped
½ teaspoon curry powder
¼ teaspoon mixed herbs
salt and pepper to taste
1 tablespoon skimmed milk

1) Place the pork, onion, curry powder, mixed herbs, salt
   and pepper in a basin and mix well. Stir in the milk.
2) Divide the meat into two and, using damp hands, shape
   into two burgers.
3) Place the burgers on the rack of a grill pan and cook under
   a hot grill, turning once, until cooked through and
   browned, about 5 minutes each side.

Exchanges per serving: 4 Protein
                        ½ Vegetable
                        5 Optional Calories

Oriental Style Pork

Serves 2 **295 Calories per serving**

2 x 5oz (150g) pork escalopes
½ clove garlic, crushed
½ teaspoon sugar
2 tablespoons soy sauce
2 tablespoons dry white wine
½" (1cm) slice peeled root ginger, finely chopped
2 teaspoons vegetable oil
1 kiwifruit, peeled and sliced

1) Lay the pork escalopes on a plate.
2) Mix the garlic, sugar, soy sauce, wine and half the
   chopped ginger together. Pour over the pork, cover and
   leave in the cool to marinade for 40-50 minutes, basting
   with the marinade from time to time.
3) Drain the pork and reserve the marinade. Place the pork
   on a rack of a grill pan and cook under a hot grill, turning
   once until rare.
4) Heat the oil in a non stick frying pan. Sauté the escalopes
   for about 1 minute, turning once.
5) Boil the reserved marinade in a small saucepan for
   1 minute, add the kiwifruit and heat through.
6) Arrange the escalopes on a warm serving plate and spoon
   over the kiwifruit marinade. Sprinkle over the reserved
   chopped ginger.

Exchanges per serving: 4 Protein
                        1 Fat
                        ½ Fruit
                        20 Optional Calories

Pork on a Bed of Cabbage

Serves 2   315 Calories per serving

10oz (300g) minced pork
1 medium onion, chopped
2oz (60g) mushrooms, chopped
1 tablespoon lemon juice
½ teaspoon mustard powder
good pinch of sage
1 tablespoon chopped fresh parsley
2 tablespoons skimmed milk
4 teaspoons seasoned flour
1lb (480g) cabbage, shredded
salt
1 teaspoon soy sauce
1 lemon, cut into 4 wedges

1) Mix the pork, onion, mushrooms, lemon juice, mustard, herbs and milk together in a bowl. Divide into 4 and shape into balls using dampened hands.

2) Sprinkle the seasoned flour onto a board, roll the balls of pork on it then transfer to a rack standing in an overproof dish. Bake at 375F/190C/Gas 5 for about 30-35 minutes or until browned and cooked through.

3) Meanwhile cook the cabbage in a saucepan of boiling water. Do not overcook as the cabbage should remain crisp. Drain well and toss in the soy sauce.

4) Spread the cabbage over a warm serving plate, arrange the pork on top and place a lemon wedge between each pork ball.

Exchanges per serving: 4 Protein
                       3½ Vegetable
                       25 Optional Calories

Sweet and Sour Ham

Serves 1   215 Calories per serving

2 slices (4oz/120g) canned pineapple with
    2 tablespoons juice
3 x 1oz (30g) slices ham
4fl oz (120ml) tomato juice
2 teaspoons cornflour

1) Cut the pineapple into small pieces.

2) Lay the ham slices flat and divide the pineapple evenly between the slices. Roll up and secure with cocktail sticks. Place in a small ovenproof dish.

3) Heat the tomato juice in a small saucepan.

4) Blend the pineapple juice into the cornflour, pour into the tomato juice and bring to the boil stirring all the time. Reduce the heat and simmer for 1-2 minutes.

5) Pour the tomato sauce over the ham rolls and bake at 375F/190C/Gas 5 for 15-20 minutes.

Exchanges per serving: 1½ Fruit
                        3 Protein
                        20 Optional Calories

Ham and Cabbage Hotpot

Serves 4   **165 Calories per serving**

4 teaspoons margarine
1 clove garlic, finely chopped
1 medium onion, chopped
8oz (240g) ham, cut into 1" (2.5cm) cubes
3oz (90g) mushrooms, sliced
1lb (480g) cabbage, shredded
9oz (270g) carrots, thickly sliced
¼ teaspoon caraway seeds
1 bay leaf
¼ teaspoon salt
¼ teaspoon pepper
¾ pint (450ml) beef stock, made with 1 stock cube
1 tablespoon cornflour

1) Melt the margarine in a large saucepan. Add the garlic and onion and sauté until the onion is transparent. Stir in all the ingredients except the beef stock and cornflour and sauté for a further 5-6 minutes.

2) Blend a little of the stock into the cornflour to form a smooth paste, put to one side.

3) Stir the remaining stock into the ham and cabbage mixture, bring to the boil, reduce the heat, cover and simmer, stirring from time to time for 30 minutes.

4) Add the cornflour paste, stir well for 3-4 minutes until the mixture boils and thickens. Remove the bay leaf and serve.

Exchanges per serving: 1 Fat
                        2½ Vegetable
                        2 Protein
                        10 Optional Calories

Ham with Sweet Potato

Serves 2   **225 Calories per serving**

1 teaspoon vegetable oil
3oz (90g) slices ham
2 canned pineapple slices (4oz/120g)
6oz (180g) cooked sweet potato, mashed
½ teaspoon soft brown sugar
¼ teaspoon ground cinnamon
2 teaspoons margarine

1) Grease two small individual ovenproof dishes with the oil.

2) Lay the ham slices in the dishes and top each with a slice of pineapple.

3) Spread the mashed sweet potato over the top and sprinkle with the sugar and cinnamon. Dot the margarine over the topping and bake at 350F/180C/Gas 4 for about 20 minutes until completely heated through.

Exchanges per serving: 1½ Fat
                        3 Protein
                        ½ Fruit
                        1 Bread
                        5 Optional Calories

Meatball Mix Up

Serves 2   **340 Calories per serving**

10oz (300g) lean minced beef
1 tablespoon vegetable oil
1 clove garlic, finely chopped
$\frac{1}{4}$″ (5mm) slice root ginger, finely chopped
4oz (120g) broccoli
4oz (120g) cauliflower
4oz (120g) green beans, sliced
4oz (120g) courgettes
$\frac{1}{2}$ teaspoon sugar
1 tablespoon soy sauce
4 teaspoons red wine
6 tablespoons water
1 teaspoon cornflour

1) Form the mince into small balls with dampened hands, place on the rack of a grill pan and grill for 6-8 minutes, turning to brown all sides.
2) Break the broccoli and cauliflower into florets, chop the stalks into $\frac{1}{2}$″ (1cm) pieces.
3) Heat the oil in a large non-stick pan, add the garlic and ginger to the pan, sauté for $\frac{1}{2}$-1 minute. Add the broccoli, cauliflower, beans and courgettes. Stir-fry 2-3 minutes.
4) Add the sugar, soy sauce, wine, 5 tablespoons water and the meatballs. Cover and simmer for 10 minutes.
5) Blend the remaining water into the cornflour to form a smooth paste, stir into the meatball mixture and bring to the boil, simmer until the mixture thickens.

Exchanges per serving: 4 Protein
$1\frac{1}{2}$ Fat
$2\frac{1}{2}$ Vegetable
20 Optional Calories

Chilli Con Carne

Serves 2   **215 Calories per serving**

1 tablespoon tomato purée
$\frac{1}{2}$ pint (300ml) beef stock, made with a stock cube
1 medium onion, chopped
$\frac{1}{4}$ clove garlic, crushed
4oz (120g) cooked minced beef
6oz (180g) cooked red kidney beans
chilli powder to taste
salt and pepper to taste
2 teaspoons cornflour
2 tablespoons water

1) Stir the tomato purée into the stock, pour into a saucepan. Add the onion and garlic and simmer until the onion is soft.
2) Stir in the beef, beans and seasonings, cover and simmer for 10 minutes.
3) Blend the cornflour to a paste with the water. Stir the cornflour paste into the meat and simmer for 1-2 minutes until the mixture thickens, stirring all the time.

Exchanges per serving: $\frac{1}{2}$ Vegetable
3 Protein
15 Optional Calories

Oriental Beef

Serves 2 **360 Calories per serving**

10oz (300g) braising steak
2 teaspoons vegetable oil
1 clove garlic, finely chopped
1 medium onion, chopped
2 sticks celery, chopped
8oz (240g) can pineapple pieces,
  drained and juice reserved
½ pint (300ml) beef stock, made
  with ½ a stock cube
2 teaspoons cornflour
1 teaspoon soft brown sugar
2 teaspoons wine vinegar
2 teaspoons soy sauce

1) Remove any visible fat from the steak and lay on the rack of a grill pan, cook under a hot grill until browned turning once, 6-8 minutes. Cool then cut into 1" (2.5cm) cubes.

2) Heat the oil in a frying pan, add the garlic, onion and celery and sauté 3-4 minutes.

3) Place the beef, vegetables, pineapple juice and stock into a casserole dish. Cover and bake at 325F/160C/Gas 3 for 1½ hours or until the meat is tender.

4) In a small bowl mix the cornflour, sugar, vinegar and soy sauce together, stir into the casserole with the pineapple pieces. Cover and return to the oven for a further 20-30 minutes.

Exchanges per serving: 4 Protein
                        1 Fat
                        1 Vegetable
                        1 Fruit
                        20 Optional Calories

Steak Roll

Serves 2 **305 Calories per serving**

13oz (390g) braising steak, cut in one slice
2 tablespoons chopped spring onions
3oz (90g) mushrooms, chopped
1 medium tomato, blanched, skinned and chopped
2 tablespoons red wine
¼ teaspoon dried mixed herbs
salt and pepper to taste
1 teaspoon English mustard

1) Lay the steak between two sheets of baking parchment and beat well with a rolling pin or steak mallet until ¼" (5mm) thick.

2) Mix together the spring onions, mushrooms and tomato, stir in the red wine, herbs and seasonings.

3) Spread the steak with the mustard, top with an even layer of the vegetable mixture. Roll up like a Swiss roll and secure with skewers.

4) Place the meat roll on a rack in an ovenproof dish, cover with the foil and bake at 375F/190C/Gas 5 for 1 hour. Remove the foil and cook for a further 15-20 minutes to brown. Drain off any excess liquid and divide into two portions.

Exchanges per serving: 5 Protein
                        2½ Vegetable
                        15 Optional Calories

Gingered Beef

Serves 2   **335 Calories per serving**

10oz (300g) rump steak
2 teaspoons vegetable oil
½ medium red pepper, seeded
    and cut into strips
½ medium green pepper, seeded
    and cut into strips
2 spring onions, sliced
2 slices root ginger, peeled and finely chopped
½ small pineapple, peeled cored and sliced
4 tablespoons water
2 teaspoons soy sauce
2 teaspoons cornflour

1) Trim any visible fat off steak and lay on the rack of a grill pan, grill until browned, turning once, cut into thin slices.

2) Heat the oil in a wok or frying pan, add the green and red peppers, spring onions and ginger, stir-fry for 2 minutes.

3) Cut the slices of pineapple in half and stir into the vegetables with the beef, cook for a further 2-3 minutes.

4) Blend the water and soy sauce into the cornflour. Add to the beef mixture and continue to stir over a moderate heat for 1-2 minutes until thickened.

Exchanges per serving: 4 Protein
                        1 Fat
                        ½ Vegetable
                        1 Fruit
                        10 Optional Calories

Steak Champignon

Serves 2   **295 Calories per serving**

1 tablespoon margarine
3oz (90g) button mushrooms, sliced
2 tablespoons red wine
3 tablespoons low-fat natural yogurt
2 x 5oz (150g) fillet or rump steak

1) Melt the margarine in a frying pan over a medium heat. Sauté the mushrooms until golden. Add the wine and cook for 2 minutes stirring all the time. Remove from the heat and stir in the yogurt, set aside.

2) Lay the steaks on the rack of a grill pan. Place under a hot grill until browned and cooked according to taste.

3) Transfer the steaks to a warm serving plate and pour over the mushroom mixture.

Exchanges per serving: 1½ Fat
                        ½ Vegetable
                        4 Protein
                        30 Optional Calories

Corned Beef Hash

Serves 1 **430 Calories per serving**

1 medium onion, chopped
4oz (120g) corned beef, chopped
¼ teaspoon dried basil
dash of hot pepper sauce
½ beef stock cube, crumbled
3oz (90g) potato, cooked and sliced
2 teaspoons margarine

1) Place the onion in a saucepan of boiling water and cook for 3-4 minutes, drain and reserve the cooking liquid.

2) Mix together the corned beef, onion, basil and pepper sauce. Spoon into a small ovenproof dish.

3) Dissolve the stock cube in 5 tablespoons of the onion water, pour over the corned beef mixture. Top with the slices of potato and dot with the margarine.

4) Bake at 375F/190C/Gas 5 for 20-30 minutes until the potato is beginning to brown.

Exchanges per serving: 1 Vegetable
4 Protein
1 Bread
2 Fat

Corned Beefburgers

Serves 2 **295 Calories per serving**

4oz (120g) corned beef
2oz (60g) fresh breadcrumbs
1 tablespoon finely chopped onion
2 eggs
1 teaspoon mustard powder
½ teaspoon dried basil
2 teaspoons flour

1) Mash the corned beef in a bowl, stir in the breadcrumbs and onion and mix well.

2) Break the eggs into a separate bowl, beat in the mustard and basil.

3) Mix the egg mixture thoroughly into the corned beef and breadcrumbs. Divide the mixture into four.

4) Sprinkle a board with the flour and shape the mixture into four burgers on the floured surface, transfer to the rack of a grill pan and cook under a hot grill for about 3 minutes each side or until crisp and golden.

Exchanges per serving: 3 Protein
1 Bread
10 Optional Calories

Stuffed Marrow

Serves 2   **275 Calories per serving**

1 medium sized marrow
2oz (60g) fresh wholemeal breadcrumbs
8oz (240g) minced veal
2 teaspoons tomato purée
2-3 tablespoons lemon juice
1 teaspoon dried mixed herbs
dash Worcestershire sauce
salt and pepper to taste
2 teaspoons margarine

1) Cut one end from the marrow and scoop out all the seeds. Peel the marrow and put to one side.
2) Mix together all the remaining ingredients, except the margarine, stir well.
3) Pack the stuffing into the marrow cavity and place the marrow in an ovenproof dish.
4) Melt the margarine and brush over the marrow, bake at 350F/180C/Gas 4 for about 1 hour or until cooked through.

Exchanges per serving: 3 Vegetable
                          1 Bread
                          3 Protein
                          1 Fat
                          5 Optional Calories

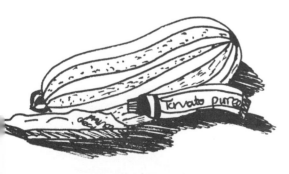

Italian Veal Stew

Serves 4   **225 Calories per serving**

8oz (240g) can tomatoes
4 teaspoons vegetable oil
4 cloves garlic, finely chopped
1¼lb (600g) boned shoulder of
    veal, cut into 1″ (2.5cm) cubes
6oz (180g) canned puréed (creamed) tomatoes
4 tablespoons dry white wine
2 sprigs of rosemary, chopped
½ teaspoon salt
pinch of pepper

1) Drain the can of tomatoes, reserve the juice; halve, seed and chop the tomatoes, put to one side.
2) Heat the oil in a large saucepan, add the garlic and veal and sauté for 3-5 minutes until the veal is browned on all sides.
3) Mix the tomatoes, reserved juice and all the remaining ingredients. Bring to the boil, reduce the heat, cover and simmer for 45-50 minutes stirring from time to time.

Exchanges per serving: 1¼ Vegetable
                          1 Fat
                          4 Protein
                          15 Optional Calories

Chicken Livers in Wine

Serves 2   **257 Calories per serving**

2 teaspoons margarine
1 medium onion, sliced
1 clove garlic, crushed
10oz (300g) chicken livers
2oz (60g) mushrooms, sliced
2 tablespoons red wine

1) Melt the margarine in a non-stick frying pan. Add the
   onion and garlic and sauté until the onion is transparent.

2) Add the chicken livers and mushrooms and sauté
   5-7 minutes.

3) Stir in the red wine and heat through. Serve piping hot.

Exchanges per serving: 1 Fat
                        1 Vegetable
                        4 Protein
                        15 Optional Calories

Chicken Liver Medley

Serves 1   **455 Calories per serving**

1½ teaspoons vegetable oil
5oz (150g) chicken livers
1 medium onion, sliced
1oz (30g) mushrooms, sliced
½ small green pepper, seeded and chopped
1 clove garlic, finely chopped
1 teaspoon plain flour
4fl oz (120ml) chicken stock,
   made with ½ a stock cube
2 tablespoons tomato purée
1 medium tomato, blanched, skinned
   and cut into wedges
3oz (90g) cooked spaghetti

1) Heat 1 teaspoon oil in a large frying pan, add the livers
   and sauté 1-2 minutes until no longer red, remove from
   the pan.

2) Add the remaining oil to the same frying pan. Add the
   onion, mushrooms, green pepper and garlic, sauté for
   1-2 minutes. Sprinkle in the flour and mix well.

3) Gradually stir in the stock and tomato purée. Bring to the
   boil and simmer for 2 minutes, stirring all the time. Add
   the tomato wedges, reserved livers and spaghetti. Cover
   and simmer 3-4 minutes until heated through.

Exchanges per serving: 1½ Fat
                        4 Protein
                        3 Vegetable
                        1 Bread
                        30 Optional Calories

Quickly Curried Liver

Serves 1   **385 Calories per serving**

1 teaspoon vegetable oil
**1 medium apple, peeled, quartered,
     cored and thinly sliced**
1 medium onion, chopped
5oz (150g) liver, cut into 2″ (5cm) strips
1 tablespoon soy sauce
¼ teaspoon curry powder

1) Heat the oil in a large non-stick frying pan. Sauté the apple and onion until the apple is soft and the onion transparent.
2) Add the liver and cook, stirring all the time, for 1-2 minutes until browned all over.
3) Add the soy sauce and curry powder and stir over a medium heat for a further 1-2 minutes.

Exchanges per serving: 1 Fat
                                        1 Fruit
                                        1 Vegetable
                                        4 Protein

Liver Pâté

Serves 1   **445 Calories per serving**

1 teaspoon margarine
1 medium onion, chopped
5oz (150g) liver, finely sliced
4 tablespoons water
2 teaspoons cornflour
2 teaspoons medium or dry sherry
3 tablespoons single cream
salt and pepper to taste

1) Heat the margarine in a frying pan, add the onion and sauté until transparent.
2) Stir in the liver and water and simmer for 4 minutes, stirring all the time.
3) Place the cornflour, sherry, cream and liver mixture into a blender, blend until smooth. Season to taste and pour into a small basin. Cover and steam for 20 minutes. Serve cold.

Exchanges per serving: 1 Fat
                                        1 Vegetable
                                        4 Protein
                              130 Optional Calories

Kidneys with Noodles

Serves 4　　　　　　　　　　**295 Calories per serving**

1¼lb (600g) lamb's kidneys
4 teaspoons margarine
1 medium onion, chopped
1 clove garlic, finely chopped
14oz (420g) can chopped tomatoes
¾ teaspoon dried basil
2 tablespoons water
2 teaspoons cornflour
12oz (360g) cooked noodles, hot
1 tablespoon chopped fresh parsley

1) Remove the outer membranes from the kidneys, cut in half lengthways and remove the core. Place on the rack of a grill pan and cook under a hot grill until browned, turning once.

2) Melt the margarine in a saucepan, add the onion and garlic and sauté 1-2 minutes, add the kidneys and brown all over stirring all the time.

3) Stir in the tomatoes and basil and bring to the boil, reduce the heat and simmer for 10-15 minutes.

4) Stir the water into the cornflour to form a smooth paste. Stir into the tomato and kidney mixture and simmer for 2-3 minutes until thickened.

5) Arrange the noodles round the edge of a warm serving plate, place the kidney mixture in the centre and serve sprinkled with parsley.

Exchanges per serving:　4 Protein
　　　　　　　　　　　　1 Fat
　　　　　　　　　　　　1½ Vegetable
　　　　　　　　　　　　1 Bread
　　　　　　　　　　　　5 Optional Calories

Stuffed Hearts

Serves 2　　　　　　　　　　**320 Calories per serving**

2 x 5oz (150g) lamb hearts
salt
2oz (60g) fresh breadcrumbs
2 x 1oz (30g) rashers lean back bacon, grilled until crisp then chopped
1 tablespoon finely chopped onion
¼ teaspoon dried mixed herbs
1 teaspoon chopped fresh parsley
2 tablespoons skimmed milk
1 tablespoon lemon juice
½ pint (300ml) beef or vegetable stock, made with ½ a stock cube

1) Wash the hearts well in cold water, remove the outer skin and any fat. Cut the dividing wall to make a single cavity. Soak in cold salted water for 1 hour, rinse well and drain.

2) Mix the breadcrumbs, bacon, onion and herbs together. Stir in the milk and lemon juice to bind.

3) Place the hearts into a small casserole, pour over the stock, cover and bake at 325F/160C/Gas 3 for 2-2½ hours or until tender.

4) Drain the hearts from the stock before serving, spoon over a little of the stock if desired.

Exchanges per serving:　4 Protein
　　　　　　　　　　　　1 Bread
　　　　　　　　　　　　105 Optional Calories

Poultry

Index

Stir-Fry Chicken

Serves 1   **320 Calories per serving**

2 teaspoons vegetable oil
4oz (120g) bean sprouts
5oz (150g) skinned and boned chicken
    breast, cut into 1″ (2.5cm) pieces
1 thin slice peeled root ginger, finely chopped
3 spring onions, sliced
1 tablespoon soy sauce
2 teaspoons clear honey

1) Heat 1 teaspoon oil in a wok or frying pan, add the bean
    sprouts and sauté 1-2 minutes. Transfer to a plate and
    keep warm.
2) Heat the remaining oil in the wok or frying pan. Add the
    chicken and ginger and stir-fry for 2 minutes.
3) Add the spring onions and continue stir-frying until the
    chicken is browned and thoroughly cooked. Stir in the soy
    sauce and honey and mix well over a medium heat for a
    further 3 minutes.
4) Top the bean sprouts with the chicken mixture and serve.

Exchanges per serving: 2 Fat
                   1½ Vegetable
                   4 Protein
                   40 Optional Calories

Tandoori Chicken

Serves 2   **195 Calories per serving**

2 x 6oz (180g) chicken portions, skinned
grated zest of ½ lemon
3 tablespoons lemon juice
½ teaspoon salt
½ teaspoon ground coriander
¼ teaspoon ground cumin
1 small onion, roughly chopped
¼″ (5mm) slice peeled root ginger
1 clove garlic
1 tablespoon paprika
5fl oz (150ml) low-fat natural yogurt
2 teaspoons vinegar
1 small carrot, cut into matchstick size strips

1) Make four cuts in each chicken portion about ½″ (1cm)
    deep.
2) Place all the remaining ingredients except the carrot in a
    blender, blend until smooth scraping down sides of the
    container as necessary.
3) Lay the chicken in a dish cover with the spiced yogurt,
    cover and leave to stand 2-4 hours, turning the chicken
    from time to time.
4) Place the chicken in an ovenproof dish, spoon over any
    remaining sauce and bake at 350F/180C/Gas 4 for
    35-40 minutes or until the chicken is cooked through.
5) Transfer the chicken to a warm serving dish and sprinkle
    with the carrot strips.

Exchanges per serving: 4 Protein
                   ½ Vegetable
                   ½ Milk

Oven Barbecued Chicken

Serves 2 **185 Calories per serving**

6fl oz (180ml) tomato juice
6 tablespoons white wine vinegar
2 teaspoons Worcestershire sauce
1½ teaspoons soft brown sugar
1 bay leaf
¼ teaspoon salt
¼ teaspoon paprika
pinch mustard powder
12oz (360g) chicken portions, skinned
1 medium onion, thinly sliced

1) Place all the ingredients except the chicken and onions in a saucepan. Bring to the boil, reduce the heat and simmer, stirring frequently, for 5-10 minutes.
2) Arrange the chicken in an ovenproof dish, lay the onion slices over the top and pour over the tomato juice sauce.
3) Bake at 350F/180C/Gas 4 for 45-55 minutes or until the chicken is cooked through. Remove and discard the bay leaf before serving.

Exchanges per serving: 4 Protein
½ Vegetable
35 Optional Calories

Foil Braised Chicken

Serves 1 **165 Calories per serving**

1 small onion, sliced
1 small tomato, sliced
2oz (60g) mushrooms, sliced
6oz (180g) chicken portion, skinned
salt and pepper to taste

1) Layer the sliced onion, tomato and mushrooms on a large square of foil.
2) Place the chicken portion on top of the vegetables and season with salt and pepper.
3) Bring the edges of the foil together to form a loose parcel. Place on a baking tray and bake at, 350F/180C/Gas 4 for 45-50 minutes or until the vegetables and chicken are tender.

Exchanges per serving: 2 Vegetable
4 Protein

Peanut Chicken

Serves 2   **300 Calories per serving**

2 teaspoons vegetable oil
12oz (360g) chicken portions, skinned
1 small onion, chopped
½ small green pepper, seeded and
   cut into thin strips
2 tablespoons crunchy peanut butter
4fl oz (120ml) chicken stock,
   made with ½ a stock cube
4 teaspoons white wine vinegar
1 teaspoon cornflour

1) Heat the oil in a non-stick saucepan over a medium heat.
Sauté the chicken pieces until well browned on all sides
and tender, remove from the pan and keep warm.

2) Add the onion and green pepper to the same saucepan.
Stir-fry for 1-2 minutes. Reduce the heat to low and stir in
the peanut butter, continue stirring until the peanut
butter has melted.

3) Blend the chicken stock and vinegar into the cornflour,
stir into the peanut butter and bring to the boil stirring all
the time.

4) Return the chicken to the saucepan and coat well in the
peanut sauce. Serve piping hot.

Exchanges per serving: 2 Fat
                      5 Protein
                      1 Vegetable
                      5 Optional Calories

Chicken and Peach Open Sandwich

Serves 1   **345 Calories per serving**

1 slice (1oz/30g) bread
1 teaspoon margarine
2 lettuce leaves, shredded
4oz (120g) cooked chicken, chopped
1 medium peach
2 teaspoons low-calorie mayonnaise
2 tablespoons low-fat
   natural yogurt
1 spring onion, chopped
1 teaspoon lemon juice
salt and pepper to taste

1) Toast the bread, spread with margarine.

2) Lay the lettuce over the toast, pile the chicken on top.

3) Dip the peach in boiling water for 30 seconds. Remove the
skin, cut the peach in half and remove the stone. Slice
thinly and arrange the slices over chicken.

4) Mix the mayonnaise with the yogurt, spring onion,
lemon juice, salt and pepper. Spoon over the chicken and
peach and serve.

Exchanges per serving: 1 Bread
                      2 Fat
                      ¼ Vegetable
                      4 Protein
                      1 Fruit
                   20 Optional Calories

Chicken Salad Medley

Serves 1   **385 Calories per serving**

4oz (120g) cooked chicken, chopped
½ medium red pepper, seeded and chopped
2″ (5cm) chunk cucumber, chopped
4oz (120g) drained canned pineapple, chopped
2 spring onions, chopped
3oz (90g) cooked long grain rice
1 tablespoon low-calorie mayonnaise
1 tablespoon lemon juice
½ teaspoon curry powder

1) Mix the chicken, red pepper, cucumber, pineapple, onion and rice together in a salad bowl.
2) Mix the remaining ingredients together. Pour over the salad ingredients and toss well. Serve lightly chilled.

Exchanges per serving: 4 Protein
                        2 Vegetable
                        1 Fruit
                        1 Bread
                        1½ Fat

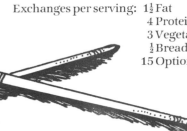

Chinese Style Chicken

Serves 2   **295 Calories per serving**

1 tablespoon vegetable oil, divided
10oz (300g) skinned and boned chicken breast, cut into ¼″ (5mm) strips
3 sticks celery, sliced
1 medium carrot, thinly sliced
2oz (60g) broccoli, chopped
1 garlic clove, finely chopped
½ teaspoon finely chopped root ginger
3oz (90g) button mushrooms, sliced
2oz (60g) spring onions, cut in diagonal slices
2oz (60g) bean sprouts
3oz (90g) drained, canned water chestnuts
4fl oz (120ml) chicken stock, made with ½ a stock cube
1 tablespoon cornflour
2 tablespoons soy sauce

1) Heat 1½ teaspoons oil in a wok or large frying pan. Sauté the chicken 2-3 minutes until lightly browned, remove from the pan.
2) Heat the remaining oil in the same pan, add the celery, carrot, broccoli, garlic and ginger, stir-fry 2-3 minutes, add the mushrooms and spring onions and stir-fry 1-2 minutes. Add the remaining vegetables and stir-fry for a further 2 minutes.
3) Blend the stock and cornflour together, add the soy sauce and stir into the vegetable mixture. Simmer 2-3 minutes, stirring all the time, until the sauce thickens.
4) Return the chicken to the pan and simmer for a further 2 minutes.

Exchanges per serving: 1½ Fat
                        4 Protein
                        3 Vegetable
                        ½ Bread
                        15 Optional Calories

Sunshine Chicken

Serves 2   **240 Calories per serving**

4 teaspoons dry white wine
8 teaspoons soy sauce
10oz (300g) skinned and boned
  chicken, cut into 1" (2.5cm) pieces
2 medium oranges
6 thin slices peeled root ginger
6fl oz (180ml) chicken stock,
  made with ½ a stock cube
2 teaspoons cornflour
½ teaspoon sugar

1) Combine the wine and soy sauce in a bowl, add the
   chicken and mix well. Cover and chill for 30-40 minutes.
2) Remove two 2" (5cm) strips of orange zest from an orange
   with a potato peeler, Cut into very fine strips about the
   size of matchsticks, reserve for garnish.
3) Peel the oranges and cut into thin slices remove any pips
   and put to one side.
4) Heat a non-stick frying pan or wok over a low heat. Add
   the chicken, the marinade and slices of ginger. Increase
   the heat and cook for about 10-12 minutes, stirring
   frequently.
5) Blend the stock into the cornflour, pour into the frying
   pan or wok and bring to the boil, stirring all the time,
   reduce the heat, stir in the sugar and simmer for about
   4 minutes.
6) Transfer the chicken pieces and sauce to a warm serving
   plate. Add the orange slices to the frying pan or wok and
   heat through, arrange around the chicken and sprinkle
   the strips of orange zest over the chicken.

Exchanges per serving: 4 Protein
                        1 Fruit
                        25 Optional Calories

Cheddar Chicken

Serves 2   **295 Calories per serving**

2 teaspoons vegetable oil
8oz (240g) skinned and boned chicken breasts
8fl oz (240ml) chicken stock, made with ½ a stock cube
1 medium carrot, cut into long thin strips
1 stick celery, chopped
1 small turnip, cut into thin strips
1 small onion, chopped
4fl oz (120ml) dry white wine
4fl oz (120ml) skimmed milk
4 teaspoons cornflour
2oz (60g) Cheddar cheese, grated
salt and pepper to taste

1) Heat the oil in a frying pan, add the chicken and cook,
   turning once, until lightly browned on both sides and
   cooked through about 4 minutes on each side.
2) Remove the chicken, place in an ovenproof dish and keep
   warm. Add the stock, vegetables and wine to the frying
   pan and simmer for 5-6 minutes until the vegetables are
   cooked and the liquid reduced by half.
3) Meanwhile prepare the cheese sauce: Gradually blend
   the milk into the cornflour. Bring to the boil, stirring all
   the time, simmer 1-2 minutes until the sauce is thick and
   smooth. Add half the cheese and stir until melted.
4) Remove the vegetables from their cooking liquid using a
   slotted spoon, spread over the chicken breasts.
5) Stir the vegetable liquid into the cheese sauce and season
   to taste. Pour over the vegetables. Sprinkle with the
   reserved cheese and place under a hot grill until lightly
   browned, 1-2 minutes.

Exchanges per serving: 1 Fat
                        4 Protein
                        1½ Vegetable
                        90 Optional Calories

Beekeepers Chicken

Serves 2 **310 Calories per serving**

10oz (300g) skinned and boned
   chicken, cut into 1" (2.5cm) pieces
1oz (30g) seasoned flour
1 tablespoon vegetable oil
3 tablespoons water
1 tablespoon clear honey
2 teaspoons lemon juice
pinch chilli powder
1 teaspoon chopped fresh chives

1) Toss the chicken in the seasoned flour to coat thoroughly.
2) Heat the oil in a non-stick frying pan or wok. Add the chicken and stir-fry until golden and tender, remove the chicken and keep warm.
3) Allow the frying pan or wok to cool a little then stir in the water, honey, lemon juice and chilli, mix well. Bring to the boil stirring all the time.
4) Stir the chicken into the honey sauce and simmer for 3-5 minutes. Transfer to a warm serving plate and sprinkle with the chopped chives.

Exchanges per serving: 4 Protein
           $\frac{1}{2}$ Bread
           $1\frac{1}{2}$ Fat
           30 Optional Calories

Turkey Croquettes with Tomato Sauce

Serves 1 **275 Calories per serving**

2oz (60g) mushrooms, finely chopped
1 tablespoon finely chopped onion
3 tablespoons skimmed milk
4oz (120g) cooked turkey, minced
1oz (30g) fresh breadcrumbs
salt and pepper to taste
1 tablespoon tomato purée
3fl oz (90ml) water
pinch ground cloves
pinch basil
1 teaspoon lemon juice
$\frac{1}{2}$ teaspoon sugar
$\frac{1}{2}$ clove garlic, crushed
pinch chilli powder
pinch salt

1) Heat the mushrooms, onion and milk in a small saucepan, simmer gently for 3 minutes.
2) Mix the turkey, breadcrumbs, salt, pepper and the mushroom mixture together. Leave to cool. Form into two croquettes.
3) Place the croquettes on the rack of a grill pan and cook under a hot grill until golden brown and heated through.
4) To make the sauce: Mix all the remaining ingredients together in a small saucepan, bring to the boil, reduce the heat and simmer for 1-2 minutes. Serve over the croquettes.

Exchanges per serving: 1 Vegetable
           4 Protein
           1 Bread
           35 Optional Calories

Turkey in Mushroom Sauce

Serves 2 **240 Calories per serving**

1 medium onion, chopped
3oz (90g) mushrooms, chopped
1 tablespoon chopped fresh parsley
juice and thinly peeled zest of ½ lemon
½ pint (300ml) chicken stock,
    made with ½ a stock cube
1 medium pickled cucumber, chopped
8oz (240g) cooked turkey, chopped
1 tablespoon cornflour
2 tablespoons water
3 tablespoons single cream

1) Place the onion, mushrooms, parsley, lemon zest and
   juice, chicken stock and pickled cucumber in a saucepan.
   Bring to the boil, reduce the heat and simmer until
   vegetables are tender.
2) Remove and discard the lemon zest. Add the turkey,
   return to the boil, simmer for a further 10 minutes.
3) Mix the cornflour with the water, stir into the turkey
   mixture and boil 1-2 minutes, stirring all the time until
   thick.
4) Remove from heat and stir in the cream.

Exchanges per serving: 1½ Vegetable
                        4 Protein
                        65 Optional Calories

Topsy Turvy Pizza Loaf

Serves 4 **305 Calories per serving**

2½ teaspoons vegetable oil
10oz (300g) turkey, minced
1 medium onion, chopped
3oz (90g) plain flour
8oz (240g) canned puréed (creamed) tomatoes
½ small green pepper, seeded and chopped
¼ teaspoon dried basil
¼ teaspoon fennel seed
3oz (90g) mozzarella cheese, grated
¼ teaspoon salt
1 egg
4fl oz (120ml) skimmed milk
1 tablespoon grated Parmesan cheese

1) Grease a 2lb (960g) loaf tin with ½ teaspoon oil set aside.
2) Heat ½ teaspoon oil in a large frying pan. Add the turkey
   and onion and stir over a moderate heat until the turkey is
   no longer pink. Mix in 1 tablespoon flour, reserve the
   remainder, and cook for 1 minute, stirring all the time.
3) Mix in the tomatoes, pepper and herbs and cook for a
   further 1-2 minutes. Spread the turkey mixture into the
   prepared loaf tin, sprinkle with the mozzarella cheese.
4) Sieve the remaining flour and salt into a bowl. Whisk
   together the egg and milk. Gradually beat into the flour to
   form a batter. Stir in the remaining oil. Pour the batter
   over the turkey mixture and sprinkle with the Parmesan
   cheese.
5) Bake at 425F/210C/Gas 7 for 25-30 minutes until puffed
   and golden.

Exchanges per serving: ½ Fat
                        3 Protein
                        ½ Bread
                        1 Vegetable
                        50 Optional Calories

Turkey Sausages

Serves 2 **175 Calories per serving**

10oz (300g) turkey, minced
¼ teaspoon salt
¼ teaspoon pepper
¼ teaspoon dried sage
good pinch ground ginger
good pinch chilli powder
1 teaspoon vegetable oil

1) Combine all the ingredients except the oil in a bowl, mix well.
2) Divide the mixture into four and using dampened hands shape to form four sausages.
3) Heat the oil in a non-stick frying pan, add the sausages and cook for about 10 minutes until browned and cooked through.

Exchanges per serving: 4 Protein
½ Fat

Chilled Turkey

Serves 2 **180 Calories per serving**

1 teaspoon vegetable oil
1 clove garlic, crushed
1 medium onion, chopped
8oz (240g) turkey, minced
8oz (240g) drained canned tomatoes, seeded and chopped
4oz (120g) canned puréed (creamed) tomatoes
4fl oz (120ml) water
2 teaspoons chilli powder
1 teaspoon Worcestershire sauce
1 teaspoon white wine vinegar
1 bay leaf
¼ teaspoon paprika
good pinch cinnamon
good pinch ground allspice

1) Heat the oil in a non-stick saucepan, stir in the garlic, onion and turkey, stir around until the turkey is browned and the onion soft, about 5 minutes.
2) Add the remaining ingredients and stir well, cook over a low heat for 25-30 minutes until thick. Remove the bay leaf before serving.

Exchanges per serving: ½ Fat
2½ Vegetable
3 Protein

Turkey and Asparagus Aspic

Serves 2　　　　　　　　　**185 Calories per serving**

6oz (180g) canned asparagus,
　drained, reserve the liquid
½ chicken stock cube, crumbled
1 tablespoon gelatine
8oz (240g) cooked turkey, chopped
6 sprigs of watercress

1) Pour the reserved liquid into a measuring jug, sprinkle in the gelatine and crumbled stock cube, stirring all the time. Stand the jug in a saucepan of simmering water until the gelatine has completely dissolved.
2) Meanwhile arrange the asparagus attractively in a 1 pint (600ml) mould. Cover with the chopped turkey.
3) Make the dissolved gelatine liquid up to ½ pint (300ml) with cold water. Pour the liquid slowly into the mould taking care not to disturb the asparagus arrangement.
4) Leave in a cool place to set. To serve; dip the mould briefly in hot water and turn out onto a serving plate. Garnish with the sprigs of watercress.

Exchanges per serving:　1 Vegetable
　　　　　　　　　　　　4 Protein

Curried Turkey Potato Topped Pie

Serves 2　　　　　　　　　**375 Calories per serving**

1 teaspoon vegetable oil
1 medium onion, finely chopped
1 teaspoon plain flour
1 tablespoon curry powder, or to taste
8oz (240g) can tomatoes
4 teaspoons tomato ketchup
½ teaspoon salt
½ teaspoon brown sugar
2 medium cooking apples,
　peeled, cored and finely chopped
8oz (240g) cooked turkey, chopped
3oz (90g) peas
6oz (180g) cooked mashed potato

1) Heat the oil in non-stick pan, sauté the onion for 2-3 minutes.
2) Stir in the flour, curry powder, mix in the tomatoes and tomato ketchup. Add the salt and sugar and simmer gently for 30 minutes, stirring frequently to prevent burning.
3) Add the apple, turkey and peas, bring to the boil, reduce the heat and simmer for 10 minutes until the apple is just soft.
4) Spoon the curry mixture into a flameproof dish, spread the mashed potato over the top and place under a hot grill to brown the top. Serve piping hot.

Exchanges per serving:　½ Fat
　　　　　　　　　　　　2½ Vegetable
　　　　　　　　　　　　1 Fruit
　　　　　　　　　　　　4 Protein
　　　　　　　　　　　　1 Bread
　　　　　　　　　　　　20 Optional Calories

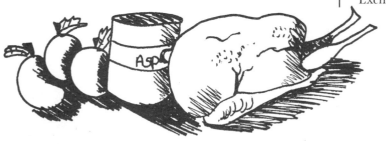

Puddings

Summer Fruit Salad

Serves 2   **105 Calories per serving**

1 medium kiwifruit
5oz (150g) strawberries
1 medium peach
4oz (120g) drained canned pineapple
  pieces with 2 tablespoons juice
1 tablespoon water
2 teaspoons clear honey

1) Peel and thinly slice the kiwifruit.
2) Halve the strawberries.
3) Halve the peach, remove the stone and dice the flesh. Mix all the fruits together.
4) Place the fruit juice, water and honey in a very small saucepan over a low heat. Stir until the honey has dissolved.
5) Pour the syrup over the fruit and chill before serving.

Exchanges per serving: 2 Fruit
                        20 Optional Calories

Peach Melba

Serves 1   **175 Calories per serving**

5oz (150g) raspberries
½ teaspoon caster sugar
1 medium peach
2oz (60g) vanilla ice cream

1) Sprinkle the raspberries with the caster sugar. Press through a sieve to form a purée.
2) Just before serving, plunge the peach in a saucepan of boiling water. Leave for 1 minute, drain and remove the skin. Cut the peach in half, remove and discard the stone.
3) Arrange the ice cream and peach halves in a dessert dish or glass, top with the raspberry purée and serve immediately.

Exchanges per serving: 2 Fruit
                        110 Optional Calories

Blackberry Fool

Serves 2   **105 Calories per serving**

5oz (150g) blackberries
2 tablespoons water
¼ pint (300ml) skimmed milk
2 tablespoons custard powder
artificial sweetener to taste

1) Place the blackberries and water in a small saucepan, cover and simmer gently for a few minutes until the blackberries are soft. Leave to cool.

2) Blend the custard powder with a little milk to form a smooth paste, and bring the rest of the milk to the boil. Pour the hot milk on to the custard powder paste, stirring all the time. Return to the saucepan and bring to the boil, stirring all the time. Boil 1-2 minutes until thick and smooth.

3) Rub the blackberries through a sieve to form a purée, discard the pips.

4) Stir the blackberry purée thoroughly into the custard, sweeten to taste. Transfer to two dessert dishes or tall glasses and chill.

Exchanges per serving: ½ Fruit
½ Milk
30 Optional Calories

Banana Split

Serves 2   **215 Calories per serving**

2 medium bananas
1 teaspoon lemon juice
4oz (120g) vanilla ice cream
1 tablespoon chocolate sauce
1½ teaspoons desiccated coconut, toasted

1) Split the bananas in half lengthways, brush all over with lemon juice.

2) Lay the bananas on two serving plates, arrange the ice cream between the banana halves.

3) Drizzle ½ tablespoon chocolate sauce over each serving and sprinkle with the desiccated coconut. Serve immediately.

Exchanges per serving: 2 Fruit
145 Optional Calories

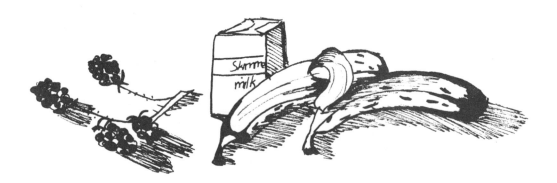

Buttermilk and Banana Whip

Serves 2   **175 Calories per serving**

2 tablespoons water
2 teaspoons gelatine
1 medium banana
1 tablespoon lemon juice
2 eggs, separated
¼ pint (150ml) buttermilk
2 teaspoons desiccated coconut, toasted

1) Pour the water into a cup, sprinkle in the gelatine stirring all the time. Stand the cup in a saucepan and leave stirring from time to time until the gelatine has completely dissolved.

2) Peel the banana, mash well or place in a blender and blend until smooth.

3) Mix the lemon juice, egg yolks and buttermilk into the banana. Place in a large bowl.

4) Stir the dissolved gelatine into the banana mixture.

5) Whisk the egg whites until peaking, carefully fold into the banana mixture.

6) Spoon the mixture into two dessert dishes or glasses and chill until set. Serve with the toasted coconut sprinkled over the top.

Exchanges per serving: 1 Fruit
                        1 Protein
                        ¼ Milk
                        10 Optional Calories

Yogurt Orange Sorbet

Serves 2   **160 Calories per serving**

2 medium oranges
10fl oz (300ml) low-fat natural yogurt
4 tablespoons water
1 tablespoon gelatine
2 teaspoons caster sugar
2 egg whites

1) Grate the zest from the oranges, stir into the yogurt.

2) Pour the water into a bowl, sprinkle in the gelatine and sugar and set the bowl over a saucepan of simmering water. Leave until the gelatine and sugar has completely dissolved, stirring from time to time.

3) Remove the bowl from the saucepan and stir in the yogurt. Leave until beginning to set.

4) In a separate bowl whisk the egg whites until peaking, fold into the setting mixture. Transfer to a shallow container and freeze.

5) To serve, remove the remaining pith from the oranges and slice or divide into segments and remove the membranes and pips. Spoon the sorbet into two glasses and arrange the orange slices or segments between spoonfuls of sorbet.

Exchanges per serving: 1 Fruit
                        1 Milk
                        40 Optional Calories

Orange Delight

Serves 2   **225 Calories per serving**

4 tablespoons undiluted low-calorie
  orange squash
1 tablespoon lemon juice
1 tablespoon gelatine
8oz (240g) low-fat soft cheese
¼ pint (150ml) buttermilk
4oz (120g) drained, canned mandarins
  with 2 tablespoons juice

1) Pour the orange squash and lemon juice into a cup.
   Sprinkle in the gelatine and stand the cup in a pan of
   simmering water. Leave until the gelatine has dissolved.

2) Place the cheese, buttermilk, mandarins and juice into a
   blender, add the dissolved gelatine and blend until smooth.

3) Divide the mixture between two dessert dishes and chill
   until set.

Exchanges per serving: 2 Protein
                        ¼ Milk
                        ½ Fruit
                        10 Optional Calories

Nutty Topped Gooseberries

Serves 2   **295 Calories per serving**

10oz (300g) gooseberries
2-3 tablespoons water
artificial sweetener to taste
2oz (60g) plain flour
¼ teaspoon ground allspice
2 tablespoons low-fat spread
4 tablespoons desiccated coconut
2 teaspoons demerara sugar

1) Top and tail the gooseberries. Place in a saucepan with
   the water and simmer for about 5 minutes until just
   tender. Stir in the artificial sweetener and transfer to a
   small ovenproof dish.

2) Sieve the flour and allspice together. Rub in the low-fat
   spread, stir in the coconut and sugar.

3) Spoon the flour mixture over the gooseberries and bake at
   375F/190C/Gas 5 for about 20 minutes until the topping
   is crisp.

Exchanges per serving: 1 Fruit
                        1 Bread
                        1½ Fat
                        80 Optional Calories

Spiced Pears

Serves 2 **65 Calories per serving**

2 medium pears
16 whole cloves
1 teaspoon lemon juice
¼ pint (150ml) water
1½ teaspoons soft brown sugar

1) Peel the pears leaving the stalks attached. Cut a very thin slice from the base so the pears stand up.
2) Press 8 cloves into each pear and stand in a small ovenproof dish.
3) Mix together the lemon juice, water and sugar. Cover and bake at 375F/190C/Gas 5 for 50 minutes or until tender. Serve hot or cold.

Exchanges per serving: 1 Fruit
15 Optional Calories

Lemon Fluff

Serves 2 **175 Calories per serving**

4 teaspoons cornflour
2 eggs, separated
2 lemons, juice and grated zest
½ pint (300ml) water
1 tablespoon gelatine
artificial sweetener to taste
6oz (180g) black grapes, halved and seeded
2 sprigs of mint

1) Place the cornflour in a large bowl, blend in the egg yolks, lemon juice and zest and stand the bowl over a saucepan of simmering water. Beat well until the mixture begins to thicken, remove from the heat.
2) Pour ¼ pint (150ml) water into a cup or small basin, sprinkle in the gelatine stirring all the time. Stand the cup in the saucepan of simmering water and leave until completely dissolved.
3) Combine the dissolved gelatine with the remaining ¼ pint (150ml) water, stir into the lemon mixture, mix well and sweeten to taste.
4) Whisk the egg whites until peaking, fold into the lemon mixture, divide between two serving dishes and chill until set.
5) Serve topped with the grapes and garnish with the sprigs of mint.

Exchanges per serving: 1 Protein
1 Fruit
20 Optional Calories

Cheesy Pineapple Pudding

Serves 2　　　　　　　　**370 Calories per serving**

2 eggs
¼ pint (150ml) skimmed milk
¼ teaspoon vanilla flavouring
artificial sweetener to taste
4oz (120g) low-fat soft cheese
6oz (180g) cooked short grain rice
4 slices (8oz/240g) canned pineapple
　　chopped, with 4 tablespoons juice
ground cinnamon to taste

1) Beat the eggs together with the milk, vanilla flavouring and artificial sweetener.
2) Add the soft cheese, rice and chopped pineapple.
3) Pour into an ovenproof dish and sprinkle with ground cinnamon. Bake at 375F/190C/Gas 5, for 35-40 minutes or until the pudding is firm and golden.

Exchanges per serving:　2 Protein
　　　　　　　　　　　　¼ Milk
　　　　　　　　　　　　1 Bread
　　　　　　　　　　　　1 Fruit

Pineapple Cheesecake

Serves 4　　　　　　　　**395 Calories per serving**

8 teaspoons margarine
8 digestive biscuits, crushed
4 tablespoons water
5 teaspoons gelatine
10oz (300g) low-fat soft cheese
juice and grated zest of 1 lemon
10fl oz (300ml) low-fat natural yogurt
8oz (240g) can crushed pineapple, drained
few drops of vanilla flavouring
artificial sweetener to taste
4 lemon slices, halved

1) Line the base of a loose based 7″ (17.5cm) round cake tin with baking parchment.
2) Melt the margarine, stir in the biscuit crumbs and press over the base of the prepared tin.
3) Pour the water into a cup, sprinkle in the gelatine, stirring all the time. Stand the cup in a saucepan of simmering water until the gelatine has completely dissolved.
4) Beat together the soft cheese, lemon juice and zest, yogurt, pineapple and vanilla flavouring. Sweeten to taste. Stir in the dissolved gelatine and spoon on to the biscuit base. Chill until set.
5) Carefully remove from the tin and serve decorated with the halved lemon slices.

Exchanges per serving:　2 Fat
　　　　　　　　　　　　2 Bread
　　　　　　　　　　　　1 Protein
　　　　　　　　　　　　½ Milk
　　　　　　　　　　　　½ Fruit
　　　　　　　　　　　15 Optional Calories

Pineapple Sponge Custard

Serves 2   **255 Calories per serving**

**4 slices (8oz/240g) canned pineapple with
  4 tablespoons juice
2 tablespoons self raising flour
2 teaspoons caster sugar
juice and grated zest of 1 lemon
2 eggs, separated
¼ pint (150ml) skimmed milk**

1) Reserve 1 slice of pineapple, chop the remaining into ½" (1cm) pieces. Arrange the chopped pineapple in a 1 pint (600ml) soufflé dish.

2) In a large bowl combine the flour and sugar.

3) Mix together the lemon juice and zest, egg yolks, milk and pineapple juice. Gradually beat into the flour and sugar to form a thin batter.

4) Whisk the egg whites until peaking, carefully fold into the batter.

5) Gently pour the batter over the chopped pineapple, place the soufflé dish in a baking tin containing 1" (2.5cm) hot water. Bake at 350F/180C/Gas 4 for 55 minutes or until golden brown and firm to touch.

6) Decorate with the reserved slice of pineapple and serve immediately.

Exchanges per serving: 1 Fruit
                             1 Protein
                             ¼ Milk
                       50 Optional Calories

Stuffed Baked Apple

Serves 1   **95 Calories per serving**

**1 medium cooking apple
2 dried dates, chopped
pinch of ground cinnamon
1 teaspoon soft brown sugar
2 tablespoons water**

1) Score around the middle of the apple with a sharp knife.

2) Remove the core, cut about ½" (1cm) off the core and press back into the base of the apple to prevent the stuffing falling out.

3) Mix together the dates, cinnamon and brown sugar. Pack into the apple and place in a small ovenproof dish.

4) Pour the water into the dish and bake at 350F/180C/Gas 4 for about 50-60 minutes until the apple is soft all the way through into the centre.

Exchanges per serving: 2 Fruit
                             20 Optional Calories

Apple Bread Pudding

Serves 1   **320 Calories per serving**

½ teaspoon margarine
1 slice (1oz/30g) white bread, cubed
1 medium apple, peeled, quartered,
    cored and chopped
8fl oz (240ml) skimmed milk
1 egg
1 teaspoon sugar
few drops vanilla flavouring
¼ teaspoon ground cinnamon
pinch ground nutmeg

1) Grease a small ovenproof dish with the margarine.
   Arrange the bread and apple in the dish.
2) Mix together the milk, egg, sugar and vanilla flavouring,
   pour over the bread and apple and leave to soak
   10-15 minutes.
3) Sprinkle with the spices and bake at 350F/180C/Gas 4 for
   35-40 minutes until the pudding is lightly browned and
   when a knife is inserted in the centre it comes out clean.
4) Remove from the oven and leave to stand 15 minutes
   before serving.

Exchanges per serving: ½ Fat
                        1 Bread
                        1 Fruit
                        ½ Milk
                        1 Protein
                        50 Optional Calories

Queen of Puddings

Serves 2   **220 Calories per serving**

¼ pint (150ml) skimmed milk
1 tablespoon caster sugar
2oz (60g) fresh white breadcrumbs
2 eggs, separated
1 tablespoon low-calorie strawberry jam

1) Warm the milk gently in a saucepan, add the sugar and
   stir until dissolved.
2) Put the breadcrumbs into an ovenproof dish, pour the
   warm milk over the bread and leave for 10-15 minutes.
   Stir in the egg yolks.
3) Bake at 350F/180C/Gas 4 for 15-20 minutes until set.
   Remove from the oven and spread the jam carefully over
   the set mixture.
4) Increase the oven temperature to 400F/200C/Gas 6.
   Whisk the egg whites until stiff but not dry. Spoon over the
   pudding drawing it up into peaks. Return to the
   preheated oven and bake for about 8 minutes or until
   golden.

Exchanges per serving: ¼ Milk
                        1 Bread
                        1 Protein
                        45 Optional Calories

Strawberry Omelette

Serves 1   **335 Calories per serving**

2 eggs, separated
2 tablespoons water
2 teaspoons caster sugar
1 teaspoon vegetable oil
5oz (150g) strawberries, hulled and sliced
2½ fl oz (75ml) low-fat natural yogurt

1) In a small bowl beat the egg yolks with the water and sugar until creamy.
2) In a separate bowl whisk the egg whites until peaking. Whisk a little white into the yolks then gently fold in remainder.
3) Heat the oil in a non-stick pan, pour the omelette mixture evenly over the base of the pan and cook until the underside is golden. Place under a hot grill until the top is golden.
4) Mix the sliced strawberries with the yogurt. Slice the omelette on to a warm plate, spoon the strawberry mixture over one half of the omelette, fold over the other half and serve at once.

Exchanges per serving: 2 Protein
                          1 Fat
                          1 Fruit
                          ½ Milk
                          40 Optional Calories

Baked Egg Custard

Serves 2   **165 Calories per serving**

½ teaspoon margarine
¼ pint (300ml) skimmed milk
2 eggs, beaten
1 tablespoon sugar
few drops of vanilla flavouring
grated nutmeg

1) Grease a small ovenproof dish with the margarine. Warm the milk in a saucepan, do not boil.
2) Whisk the eggs together with sugar and vanilla flavouring and pour into the greased dish. Grate nutmeg all over the surface.
3) Stand the ovenproof dish in a big tin of hot water. Bake at 325F/160C/Gas 3 for 25-30 minutes until just set. Test to check the custard is set by gently placing a knife down the centre of the custard then press each side of the cut very gently, no liquid should squeeze out.

Exchanges per serving: ½ Milk
                          1 Protein
                          45 Optional Calories